Biblia's Guide to Warrior Librarianship

Humor for Librarians Who Refuse to Be Classified

Written by Amanda Credaro

Illustrated by Peter Lewis

2003
Libraries Unlimited, Inc.
A Member of Greenwood Publishing Group, Inc.
Westport, Connecticut

LIBRARIES UNLIMITED, INC.
A MEMBER OF GREENWOOD PUBLISHING GROUP, INC.
88 Post Road West
Westport, Connecticut 06881
1-800-225-5800
www.lu.com

Library of Congress Cataloging-in-Publication Data

ISBN 1-59158-002-1   CIP

Biblia's Guide to Warrior Librarianship

Humor for Librarians Who Refuse to Be Classified

Contents

What's Inside:

Of Special Interest...

FEATURING

...and not to be missed!

To my long-suffering family,
who already knew both the joys and
sorrows of having a Warrior Librarian
as wife and mother, and then had to
adjust to the addition of the
birth of a book...

Foreword

Fresh from her conquest of the Internet, Biblia the Warrior Librarian is now taking on the world of print. Most Internet superstars have done it the other way around, but Biblia follows her own path. It is not so much that she hears a different drummer; rather that her drummer uses music provided by Biblia.

Along the way, Biblia has acquired a great deal of experience, not to mention wisdom, which she shares with friends and enemies alike through this book. To the new librarian going into a first job interview, she says: "Leave all your weapons at home ... refrain from biting, kicking, punching, or otherwise injuring your interviewer, at least until after you've been appointed to the position." After that, though, for warrior librarians, it's open season–on administrators who don't understand libraries, on patrons with overdue books, on booksellers who arrive without an appointment, and on "loud animals" who visit the library for purely conversational purposes. Biblia's strategies are guaranteed (by Biblia, though the book does include some caveats—note them well).

Biblia has also found time in her busy life to ponder the great issues facing our profession today, and we benefit. What should library schools be teaching to potential warrior librarians? What statistical techniques can be used to improve a library's borrowing figures? How can people search the OPAC during a power outage? And last but not least, how can a librarian "amuse 478 small, wet children for 57 minutes during a rainy lunchtime in a school library built to seat 60" when the librarian is equipped only with "one pair of scissors, some sticky tape, and a fire extinguisher"?

Friends of Biblia's Warrior Librarian website will find their favorite stories in this book—-and many new ones as well. For people who are meeting Biblia for the first time, enjoy the fun (but stand at least one sword's length back!).

L. Anne Clyde, Professor
Library and Information Science
The University of Iceland
Reykjavik, Iceland

Be Sure to Check out the Official Warrior Librarian website. And, the work of Illustrator Peter Lewis can be found at his website:

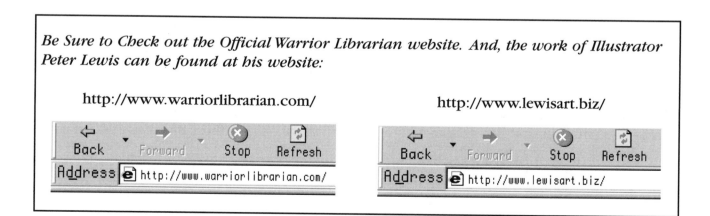

http://www.warriorlibrarian.com/   http://www.lewisart.biz/

Preface

The question no one has asked is "What is Warrior Librarianship?" Perhaps this is because it is self-evident. Many readers will know that this book started out as a website and grew from there. There are not many digital documents that can claim to be too big for the Internet, so I guess that this is another first for Warrior Librarianship. Not that the quantity exceeded any server capacity but only in the need to be even more accessible for that most literate of the educated community, librarians.

Comments left in the guestbook at the Warrior Librarian Weekly website demonstrate that Warrior Librarianship is equally applicable to all types of librarians, regardless of their library's settings. Academic, special, school, public, corporate, research, and a whole truckload that are unfamiliar to me— all librarians seem to find something there to which they can relate. Warrior Librarianship also seems to be location independent, with critical acclaim (but sadly no money) coming from all the major continents and quite a few islands. The big surprise was the messages of encouragement from library school academics. I guess they've all been where most of us are now.

However, conspicuous by their absence are any messages from library administrators. I just know they are out there somewhere, lurking in the dark recesses of their offices, waiting for me to apply for vacant positions in their libraries. It is then that they will have their vengeance. As Alfred Hitchcock said, "Revenge is a dish best served cold." I agree—I've served a lot of it in my time, and it's much better that way. But don't leave it in the back of the refrigerator; it gets moldy after a while, and you have to throw it away.

But I digress. This book includes the most popular of the items from the website but expands on the original content. The other pieces in this book were specifically written for print publication. Similarly, this book contains cartoons that are not available on the website.

Being treeware, there are no lengthy operating instructions. You don't need to attend any tutorials to operate this book, online or otherwise. Not being a strictly linear work of literature, you don't need to start at the first page on boot-up. The registration card has been omitted because no one ever sends them in anyway (then they wonder why they missed out on the free upgrade).

Reader Agreement

It is vitally important that you do NOT read this book while operating heavy machinery. No responsibility is accepted for damage caused to your life or kidneys in using this book. The user accepts all responsibilities and releases from responsibility the author, illustrator, publisher, booksellers, and anyone else who in any way assisted you in obtaining this book.

If you agree to the above conditions of use, you must now turn the page to continue using this book. If you do not agree, you will need to fold the front of the book over this page, in a technical operation known as 'closing'.

Acknowledgments

A multitude of people deserves thanks and praise, but I am long out of practice at such social skills. First and foremost, thanks to my family, who had to become not only invisible but also silent (if not absent). It's always nice to meet new people, and because I've hardly spoken to any of them for such a long time, they've all changed a lot. I'll let them take their name tags off in a few weeks.

Peter Lewis, illustrator extraordinaire, proved to be a valuable colleague and a reciprocal source of inspiration. Of course, in return he was introduced to the mystical world of librarians in general and the idiosyncrasies of Warrior Librarianship in particular. I am in his debt—literally. I hope enough of these books will be sold to cover his expenses, with perhaps a bit left over for his family to get name tags as well.

Of the staff at Libraries Unlimited, especially deserving of mention are Sharon Coatney, who basically left me alone and let me get on with writing the book; Carmel Huestis, who led the production team in the early evolution of the book; Joan Garner (Joan Garner Art Design) who did such a great job of layout—many times over; and possibly most importantly, Edward Kurdyla, who signs the checks.

Many thanks also to Professor Anne Clyde for her kind words in the foreword to this book. She has been an active advocate of Warrior Librarianship since its inception.

Actually, the first invitation to write the foreword went to James H. Billington, the Librarian of Congress. He wrote a very nice letter back, saying he was unable to write the foreword. I guess he was so overcome with laughter that his eyes were watering too much to read any more. Now that's what I call a great sense of humor.

The fight against the stereotyping of librarians has had a web presence for quite a while, and a whole conference of librarians has demonstrated its angst in a correspondingly large variety of forms. Many thanks to Linda Absher (the Lipstick Librarian) for allowing her *Beauty Tips for Librarians* to be reproduced, and also Peter Hughes (a quiet, unassuming genius in many fields, including school librarianship) for giving permission to include his *Pointers for Teachers* here.

Libel laws being such as they are, I can't specifically name those who showed me the path to Warrior Librarianship. Without their blinkered, uncomprehending ignorance—and their insistence in sharing it—I would never have realized the need to articulate the finer points of our profession. And, without the necessary accompanying reflection, I would not have been able to see the humorous aspects of our daily working lives as information professionals. So, I guess it's only proper that I give them begrudging thanks and refrain from the usual nonverbal signals, at least for the moment.

Amanda Credaro
[aka, Biblia, the Warrior Librarian]
Sydney, Australia

Part 1 BECOMING A LIBRARIAN

Guidelines for Choosing Your Library School

ADMISSION REQUIREMENTS

Admission requirements are established by the institution and the school. Although they vary from program to program, generally a bachelor's degree from an accredited institution and a minimum grade point average of 3.0 on a 4.0 scale (or equivalent, such as a B average) is required.

If you can't meet the minimum requirements, you should insist that the course of your choice must consider your special circumstances. If you don't have anything compelling enough, try laying on the floor and crying—particularly if the selection committee is male-dominated, and you are female.

CURRICULUM

Considerable variation exists in curricula offered by the programs, such as the number and types of required (or core) courses. The number of academic credit hours required for a master's degree also varies from 36 semester hours to 72 quarter hours. Some schools emphasize full-time studies, whereas others have a larger percentage of part-time students; however, most have a time limit for completing a degree.

You should look for a course that is infinitely flexible because you never know what things life may throw at you.

FACULTY

A school's catalog or website usually lists names of full-time and part-time faculty, often with their degrees and specializations. You may want to check the professional affiliations, publications, and areas of research of faculty members teaching in your areas of interest.

More important, this will give you a head start in private investigations that will continue to ensure high grades should you select the school where the faculty has the most skeletons in the closet.

FINANCIAL AID

This is the primary consideration in choosing a school. Most financial aid is in the form of scholarships, teaching and research assistantships, grants, work-study programs, loans, and/or tuition assistance. The school and others administer some financial aid opportunities through the general university financial aid office. There may be reciprocal tuition agreements between states that can reduce tuition or provide tuition waivers. In addition, some employers provide tuition assistance as a fringe benefit to employees.

Ask around, especially if you have outstanding grades and are not a sports star. You might find there are unpublished sources of funding available. Failing that, see under "Faculty" above.

The Inkblot Test

Look at each of the ink blots below to see which library specialization would suit your personality best:

Ink Blot

LOOKS LIKE A:

THEN YOU SHOULD CONSIDER A CAREER IN:

Set of Dewey numbers →	Cataloging
Set of letters →	Systems architecture
Computer keyboard →	Database management
Farm animals →	Janitorial duties

Ink Blot

LOOKS LIKE A:

THEN YOU SHOULD CONSIDER A CAREER IN:

Apple →	School librarianship
Macintosh computer →	Web page managements
Mattisse painting →	Photo archivist
Buttocks →	Adult services librarianship

Ink Blot

LOOKS LIKE A: **THEN YOU SHOULD CONSIDER A CAREER IN:**

Ashtray	Knowledge integration
Party invitation	Academic librarianship
Orchestra	Music librarianship
Budget statement	Government documents

Ink Blot

LOOKS LIKE A: **THEN YOU SHOULD CONSIDER A CAREER IN:**

Mailbox	Document delivery
Telephone	Remote services
Computer	Network administration
Truck	Outreach librarianship

Ink Blot

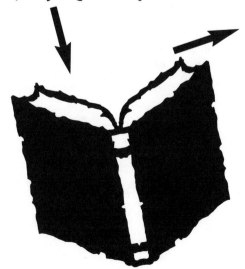

LOOKS LIKE A: **THEN YOU SHOULD CONSIDER A CAREER IN:**

Dictionary	Reference librarianship
Computer manual	Electronic services
Checkbook	Acquisitions supervision
Desert island	Library administration

University of REAL LIFE

MASTER OF LIBRARY SCIENCE

COURSE DETAILS

CORE TOPICS

LIS 101 Introduction to Digital Information Technologies
This course includes basic operation of simple computers, hardware and software maintenance, operating system design and construction, and a list of really useful excuses to explain to patrons why things don't work.

LIS 102 Introduction to Library and Information Science
Introduction to the history, purpose, functions, and processes of the field; its place in society; practice of the profession in various types of settings; and alternative courses for those who realize it's not all about stamping things.

LIS 103 Information Sources and Services
Overview of information access and delivery, types of resources and formats used in information services, and action research project into the completely inane methodology used by the majority of library users to find information. Students are advised to give up all social life.

LIS 104 Introduction to Knowledge Organization
Basic principles of bibliographic control. Emphasizes understanding the function of catalogs, indexes, bibliographies, web browsers and acquiring the ability to use and interpret these tools effectively. Introduction to bibliographic utilities, online catalogs and indexes, world wide web, metadata and Dublin Core, MARC formats, Anglo-American Cataloging Rules, Library of Congress Subject Headings, Sears List of Subject Headings, Dewey Decimal Classification, and Library of Congress Classification. *Prerequisites: Satisfactory completion of both medical and psychological evaluation.*

LIS 105 Internship
One hundred twenty hours during a semester at an approved site. Students augment what they have been taught in formal courses, further their career objectives, enhance their skills, fantasize about their achieving head librarian status, and gain a completely unrealistic view of library operation.

ELECTIVES

LIS 201 Management of Libraries and Information Centers
Focuses management theory on organizing for library and information services, conducting a legal bag search, reducing theft, and managing personal stress.

LIS 202 Records Management I: Fundamentals
Principles and techniques in paper shredding, photocopying, and filing are examined. Another really useful list is provided to explain any missing documents.

ELECTIVES

LIS 203 Information Networks
An examination of various forms of cooperation and resource sharing, particularly as facilitated by telecommunications networks in providing information services, relative merits of various library organizations and their annual conference locations, and interpreting Bulletin Board messages and cryptic emails.

LIS 204 Electronic Resources of the Internet
An introduction to global information systems and resources available through networks linked by the Internet, particularly as used for information storage, access, delivery, resource sharing, and communication as they affect the information professions. Hot-spots for patron web-surfing, downloads, and chat rooms.

LIS 205 Humanities Sources and Services
A study of the nature of the knowledge, historical development, research, and publications in the humanities. Includes the identification and evaluation of bibliographic, reference, and selection sources in philosophy, religion, language, fine arts, minor and applied arts, performing arts, music, and world literature. Learn to differentiate between pornography and art and to determine what will be acceptable to library administrators.

LIS 206 Young Adult Sources and Services
A survey of adolescents and their reading, with special emphasis on books written especially for this age group (12–18), together with research explaining why they'd rather play computer games.

SCHOOL LIBRARY SPECIALIZATION

LIS 311 School Media Centers
An examination of principals' management styles and strategies for manipulating policy documents in the media center's favor. This course examines lack of understanding by administrators related to policy development, budgeting, personnel, resources organization, networking, public relations, and facilities planning.

LIS 312 General Methods of Teaching
A study of generic instructional techniques, during which the MLS student begins to understand why the development of a repertoire of methodologies and materials will make no difference to attitudes of learners.

LIS 313 School Media Materials and the Curriculum
Survey of nonfiction resources in support of the subject content areas in the modern school curriculum. Attention is given to new developments in the curriculum, with emphasis on the whole language approach as it relates to the selections and use of library materials, which your budget will never allow you to purchase.

GENERAL LIBRARIANSHIP

LIS 301 Interactive and Hyperactive Library Users
Review of research, resources, concepts, and principles of human-computer interaction pertinent to the behavior of library users. Compares software and hardware available for patron entertainment.

LIS 302 Introduction to Preservation
An introduction to the principles and practices of keeping your job. Current preservation methods; national, regional, and local preservation efforts; the history of preservation; and early retirement options will be examined.

LIS 303 Master's Project
Independent research, design, or development that may include one of the following: a research paper of publishable quality, an instructional or informational design program, or a creative performance program. The student will be required to present a proposal for approval as well as the completed results of the selected paper or program project to to the faculty adviser, the project supervisor, and the dean. *Submissions contaminated with human blood will not be accepted.*

LIS 697 Master's Thesis
Independent research for the preparation, development, and presentation of a master's thesis under a faculty member's advisement and supervision. The completed thesis must be approved by the thesis adviser and the dean and must be accompanied by a sizable donation to the dean's retirement fund.

 # Vital Latin Phrases for Librarians

SITUATION	RESPONSE	TRANSLATION
For patron offering lame excuses about a damaged book:	Re vera, cara mea, mea nil refert.	Frankly, my dear, I don't give a damn.
Patron: "You said that I could have [blank] book today. You even wrote it down in that book. This is the third time I've asked for it. I want to see someone in charge."	Te audire no possum. Musa sapientum fixa est in aure.	I can't hear you. I have a banana in my ear.
Patron: "I can't find it. It wasn't where you said it was."	Stultus est licut stultus facit.	Stupid is as stupid does.
Patron queries directions numerous times:	Amicule, deliciae, num is sum qui mentiar tibi?	Baby, sweetheart, would I lie to you?
Previous patron returns, asks same question again:	Puto vos esse molestissimos.	I think that you are very annoying.
Patron states: "This book sucks."	Nullus est liber tam malus ut non aliqua parte prosit.	There is no book so bad that it is not profitable in some part. (Pliny Minor).
On sending out overdue notices:	Lege atque lacrima.	Read 'em and weep.
On having to eject a patron:	Es debilem vinculum, vale!	You are the weakest link, goodbye!
On being confronted by a huge backlog of cataloging/shelving/processing/etc.:	Veni, vidi, volo in domum redire.	I came, I saw, I want to go home.
In response to having a mistake pointed out to you:	Nemo mortalium omnibus horis sapit.	No mortal is wise all the time.
In response to general abuse or name-calling:	Nihil est—in vita priore ego imperator Romanus fui.	That's nothing—in a previous life I was a Roman emperor.
To obnoxious young patrons:	Antiquis temporibus, nati tibi similes in rupibus ventosissimis exponebantur ad necem.	In the good old days, children like you were left to perish on windswept crags.
To obnoxious older patrons:	Caesar si viveret, ad remum dareris.	If Caesar were alive, you'd be chained to an oar.
To patron indicating indifference about threatened ejection, fines, or other penalties:	Postatem obscuri lateris nescitis.	You do not know the power of the dark side.

SITUTATION	RESPONSE	TRANSLATION
To colleagues, announcing a coffee break when patrons are present:	Nunc est bibendum.	Now we must drink.
Notice to place over Internet-connected computers:	Caveat Despascor!	Browser Beware!
Signs for mail sorting trays:	Purgamentum Init, Exit Purgamentum.	Garbage in, Garbage out.
To be whispered to a colleague in times of trouble:	Quando omni flunkus moritati.	When all else fails, play dead.
In response to any general complaint:	O curas hominum! O quantum est in rebus inane!	Ah, human cares! Ah, how much futility in the world!
To anyone complaining about your use of Latin:	Vah! Denuone Latine loquebar? Me ineptum. Interdum modo elabitur.	Oh! Was I speaking Latin again? Silly me. Sometimes it just sort of slips out.
To anyone responding in Latin:	Abutebaris mondo subjunctivo.	You've been misusing the subjunctive.
On being reprimanded by supervisor for using Latin to abuse patrons:	Diabolus fecit, ut id facerem!	The devil made me do it!

NOTE: Revera linguam latinam vix cognovi.

Self Defense for Librarians

HALITOSIS BLOCK
For reference queries by patrons with bad breath, this blocking maneuver will allow you simultaneously to answer the phone, scan barcodes, and maintain a comfortable distance from the offender.

ADVANCING CLIMB
Progress up the corporate ladder by lifting yourself up over colleagues. This technique requires strength, determination, courage, and a complete absence of personal and professional ethics.

FINANCE GRAPPLE

When budget cuts threaten your job security, it is important to wrestle down the human resources director or whoever is in charge of staffing. By forcefully pointing out your contribution to the success of the library, it is obvious that your services will continue to be required.

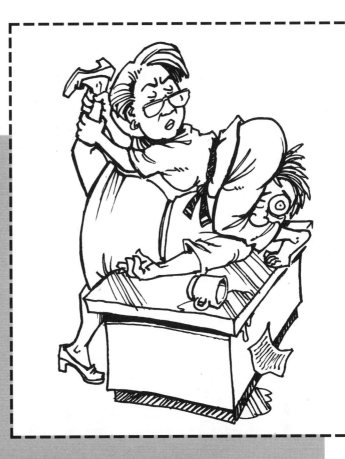

BACKSTAB BLOCK

Prevent unnecessary pain and suffering by blocking rear attacks that use slander, innuendo, derision, or other forms of abuse.

WAVE AND STAMP

Handy technique for greeting colleagues or friends while you are busy at the circulation desk. Potentially violent patrons will take notice of your stance and rethink their intended behavior.

more

ATTENTION GRABBING
You can't issue instructions to subordinates, explain problems to superiors, or help patrons if they aren't listening. This simple technique makes sure you have their undivided attention and also checks the battery connections in hearing aids.

SPIDER KILL
Some really gruesome livestock crawling up the wall? Yechhh! Don't be tempted to hit it with a book (at least not one of your own), but remove all danger—real or perceived—with this high kick.

DOWNWARD FOOT STOMP
If you've been unable to make your point, a demonstration of your innermost feelings is appropriate. Rather than folding your arms and pouting, a really definite stomp is in order—particularly if you can connect with the foot of the object of your angst.

Preservation Techniques
(14) Defense for Librarians
Self

➤ Suggested Research Topics for Higher Degrees in Library Science ◀

➤ The psychodynamics of patron-librarian interactions: destructive effects of power inequalities.

➤ A comparison of behavioral responses to anxiety between information professionals in different types of libraries: basket cases in different places.

➤ The social and interpersonal processes in providing young adult library services: every librarian's nightmare.

➤ Perceptions of success outcomes and the effects of payment on satisfaction in recovery of overdue materials.

➤ The interactions between academic stress, coping and cognitive appraisals and attribution, self-esteem, and depression imposed by stereotyping of librarians.

➤ Incorporating C into $Si_{1-x}Ge_x$ epitaxial layers: a study on improving borrowing statistics through numerical manipulation.

➤ Quarto books and the link with lithospheric deformation on the northern margin of the Australian continent.

➤ Nonequilibrium surface tension phenomenon observed in library patron search strategies: no, we don't have that book.

➤ Characterizing the prediction uncertainty of data-based models for multiple use libraries: you can make me but never break me.

➤ The fluid dynamics and sedimentology of borrower eating habits: more than just coffee stains and cake crumbs in returned books.

➤ Quantification and modeling of methane fluxes from library patrons: Occupational Health and Safety considerations of odor neutralizers.

➤ Use of low-powered laser ablation to enforce exit control in libraries.

➤ Investigations of reference incorporation, transport, and deposition in alpine libraries.

➤ Paleomagnetism and its effects on metal library shelving: a longitudinal study.

➤ Incorporating binaural cues in a computational model of auditory scene analysis: reference interviews in a crowded library.

Rhyming Dictionary of Librarianship

A is for after hours,

When the library is closed;
When the elves and the fairies,
Shelve books, it's supposed.

B is for backlog,

Of work to be done;
There's always a heap,
And trust me—it's not fun.

Circulation's the process,

Of borrow 'n' return;
No-brainer activity?
But the librarian's concern.

Dewey's the man

Who came up with the numbers;
For placing the books on,
Kings, cats, and cucumbers.

Empathy with patrons,

Is a skill you must learn;
If you would like,
Them all to return.

Finding aids are a help,

When searching for stuff;
Without them you'll find,
The going quite tough.

Games are quite strangely,

Shelved with the Arts;
The "seven hundred" section,
Has many strange parts.

Hypertext are the links,

Found all over the 'net;
They might take you places,
You'd rather forget.

Icons are graphics,

Found on a screen;
They represent data,
That cannot be seen.

Joint-use libraries,

Are interesting places to work;
They've sent many a librarian,
Completely berserk.

K is for knowledge,

Constructed from data;
But wisdom you gain,
Not sooner, but later.

Library routines,

Make sure that work's done;
From early morning light,
'Til the setting of sun.

Manuals are handbooks,

Full of useful instructions;
Written by people,
Unfamiliar with library obstructions.

Noddy and Big Ears,

Are now banned from our shelves;
Not politically correct,
Are some fairies and elves.

Oh! for a cuppa,

And some peace and quiet;
But every day here,
Is just like a riot.

Printers, scanners, and networks,

Are for digital access;
Their guaranteed failure,
Is cause for distress.

Quarto are big books,

Too large for small shelves;
Make room on a bookstand,
Then read them yourselves.

Reference is the section,

Of noncirculating books;
They may not be borrowed,
But are taken by crooks.

Subject headings are terms,

To find information;
Familiarity with these,
Will save much frustration.

Truncation of search terms,

Is a handy device;
But use care with your search tools,
Because some are not nice.

User services are provided,

In libraries worldwide;
Other tasks, though pressing,
Need be pushed to one side.

Vocabulary, whether free,

Or controlled by thesaurus;
Must be used with discretion,
Only patrons may cuss.

World Wide Web is a network,

Of global computers;
Giving data and info,
To digital commuters.

Xerox produced a machine,

That could copy;
But now we just use,
The trusty cheap floppy.

Young adults are readers,

Made up of our youth;
Some are quite learned,
And others uncouth.

Zzzz's are for quick naps,

For a tired librarian;
To dream of a life,
Less barbarian.

AUTHENTIC ASSESSMENT:

LIBRARIANSHIP

–FINAL EXAM–

INSTRUCTIONS: Complete all core topic questions and all questions from ONE of the options.

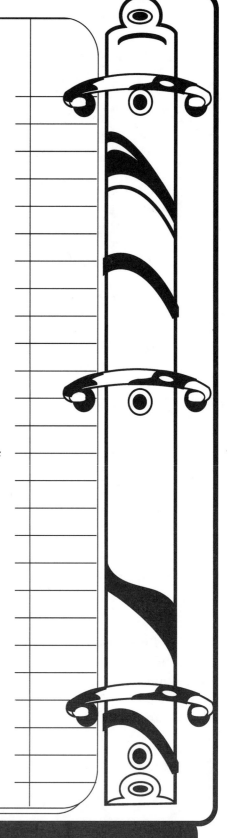

CORE TOPICS

PART A: An irate patron confronts you with a complaint about being charged for a lost book and pulls a knife on you. Outline the strategy you would use to get this person to volunteer to cover books for the library.

PART B: Design a promotional brochure for patrons expounding the virtues of a library. Include the information that very few of the resources are current and that there are no funds for new materials, but express these facts in a positive light.

PART C: Demonstrate the need for a new library at your place of work. You are restricted to the use of 20 blank pages of 45# matte paper, 6 paper clips, 2 rubber bands, and a piece of heavy earthmoving equipment of your choice.

PUBLIC LIBRARIANSHIP OPTION

PART A: The governing body of the public library has decided to form a steering committee. Without spending more than $100, draft a budget for expenditure that will guarantee your inclusion on the committee.

PART B: You are handed a roster that includes shelving, circulation, reference desk, cataloging, processing, and acquisitions, and you find that your shifts are heavily weighted toward your least enjoyable task. Develop a profile of your coworkers that identifies those most easily manipulated into swapping with you.

PART C: The head librarian has taken a noticeable dislike to you. Outline your plan for obtaining employment elsewhere, taking into account that you will not be receiving a favorable reference or recommendation.

ACADEMIC LIBRARIANSHIP OPTION

PART A: You find that the students at your institution are unable to locate even the most basic of resources. Resource and staffing constraints prevent the delivery of any bibliographic instruction. Create appropriate signage to assist these students, using words of no more than five letters, WITHOUT using the words "you," "stupid," or "dumb."

PART B: The faculty insists on receiving services before students. Although they are more constrained in verbal expressions of their outrage than students, they could place your job in jeopardy. Draw up a list of inexpensive diversions to keep the students amused while you protect your position.

PART C: Closed stack contains 285,000 items, and someone has asked for a book that you were known to have last reshelved. The item cannot be found. List six places you can hide for at least your whole shift without being discovered.

SCHOOL LIBRARIANSHIP OPTION

PART A: Explain how you would amuse 478 small, wet children for 57 minutes during a rainy lunchtime in a school library built to seat 60. The only equipment you are allowed to use is one pair of scissors, some sticky tape, and a fire extinguisher. You must include the educational outcome, a pro forma for self-assessment, and your medical insurance number.

PART B: Your principal has instructed you to improve library usage rates of the math classes at your school within the next two weeks. You will be given neither any additional funding nor extra hours of clerical support. Draft a brief memorandum to your principal, expressing your views on his or her expectations. Use Harvard referencing style.

PART C: Generate a learning experience on the use of technology for research that can be delivered during a total power outage (blackout). You must include overhead projections and a PowerPoint presentation. Your lesson should incorporate OPAC usage and an Internet search.

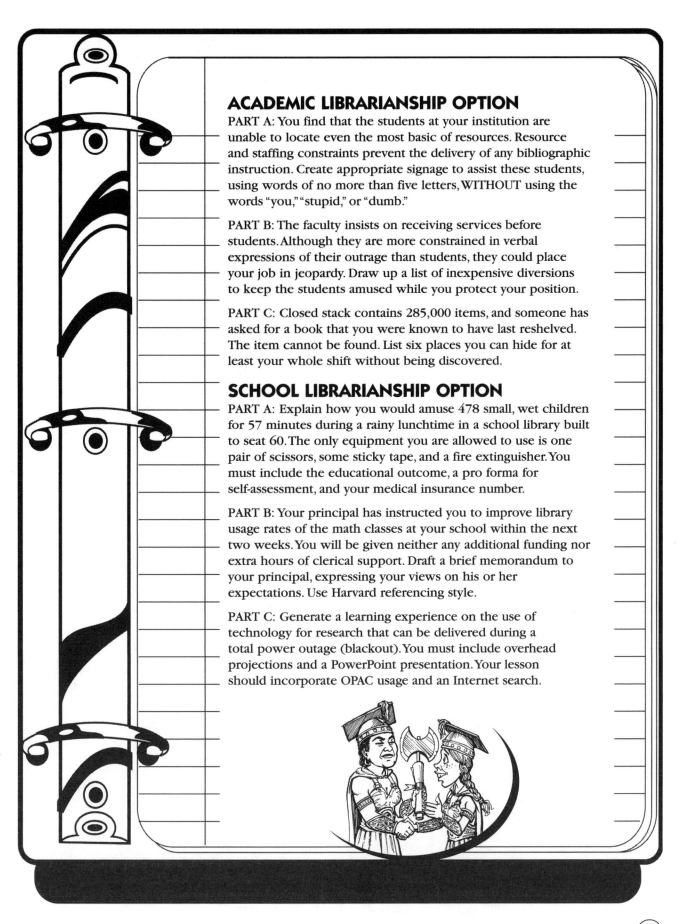

POSITIONS VACANT

LAW LIBRARY in large private company offers new information science graduate immediate placement. No prior experience necessary. Full on-the-job training provided at full salary. No out-of-hours work. Contact John or Henry on 0011-7489-3879-8494, and reverse the phone charge.

SCHOOL LIBRARY seeks qualified, innovative information professional to manage the resource centre. Unlimited budget, unlimited staffing, no administrative interference in library decisions. Modern building and all new equipment. School community committed to high academic standards. Phone: 1800-N-O-S-T-R-I-N-G-S

CUNARD LINE has six vacancies for librarians to work on round the world cruise on the Queen Elizabeth II. First class private cabin, in addition to full-scale salary. All expenses paid. No contracts - you leave when you want to. Visit our website and complete the online form. We will contact you within 24 hours. www.cruisepersonnel.com

LIBRARIAN OF CONGRESS position now vacant. All library school graduates are welcome to apply. The successful candidate's name will be pulled out of a barrel at 12 noon on November 1, 2001. Write your name and phone number on the back of an envelope, and send to FreePaid 24, Library of Congress, Washington.

PUBLIC LIBRARY in exclusive suburban area requires Reader Guidance Advisor. The successful applicant will be required to read three books (of their own choosing) a week, and write a 20 word plot summary for each. Salary US$60,000 negotiable, with bonuses for additional work. OK to work from home. Overseas applicants welcome. Apply to Sally: Golden Sands Library, CA.

POSITIONS WANTED

FORMER LIBRARY ADMINISTRATOR willing to work long hours for clerical wages in inner city public library. Happy to do shelving and book repairs in own time. Will relocate to any city, and pay own expenses. Send details to Carl at 2 Long Street, Upper Crust, Fl.

MULTI-MILLIONAIRE wants to sponsor libraries. Prefer small under-resourced rural area, but willing to support any. Indifferent as to publicity. Send all unpaid accounts to
W. Gaits,
c/- Credit Suisse
Zürich, Switzerland

BOOK SWAP PROGRAM

PUBLISHERS will swap old, worn, superseded, or unpopular books for new editions or more popular titles from current catalogs. Free service in the interests of supplying high quality resources to all libraries. Send unwanted books to American Publishers' Association

TOP $$$ PAID

OLD NEWSPAPERS wanted. Prefer ones with pictures and news items cut out or missing pages. Email us to collect - any amount from a single page to pallet loads. oldnews@crazycollectors.com

GOT A CAMERA?

PHOTOGRAPHS needed of your library. Print or digital images OK. All submissions will be published. Write to c/- this paper.

FREE COMPUTERS FOR LIBRARIES

FACTORY OVER-RUN: Pentium 4, 20GB HDD, 2GHz. Brand new. No storage space left in warehouse. Complete with 17" monitors, keyboards, etc. We will pay freight. Limit 10 per library. Phone: 1800-H-A-R-D-W-A-R-E

EXTRA INCOME. Library journal will pay for articles on any topic. $100 per 100 words. No limit. Opinion pieces, research articles, and letters to the editor all now worth money. Submissions to:
World Library Journal

CONFERENCES

5 STAR resort offers free facilities for library conferences. Accomodation at US$10 per room. We LOVE librarians. Call for a brochure.
Florida Keys Park Royal

FOR SALE

BOOKMOBILE Low miles, exce. cond., fully equipped. Cheap. More details from Internet Public Library. www.ipl.org

FIRST EDITION Gutenberg Bible. Best offer. Contact British Museum, London, England.

Warrior Librarian Weekly: Now available from all good bookshops and news agents.

Career Advice for Potential Warrior Librarians

✰ PREPARE YOUR RÉSUMÉ IN ADVANCE:

Include your name, date of birth (no cheating here), educational background, experience, goals, and ambitions. Make sure that your résumé highlights your strengths for whatever area you are applying. Operations librarians should mention the long hours they spend each night on the Internet; catalog wanna-bes should include their passion for Dewey and should mention spending each vacation cutting up the New York/London/Sydney *Times* (or their metric equivalents) and filing the clippings by an appropriate subject heading system of their own invention. Stress how superior your system is over any of the existing ones.

✰ STUDY THE LIBRARY IN ADVANCE:

Make certain that you actually WANT to work in that particular library. A good tip is first to examine a text on body language before you make your reconnaissance visit. Look out for sagging shoulders (which may indicate an extreme workload); a shuffling gait might mean long hours on your feet, and coke-bottle glasses could alert you to substandard lighting. Of course, a combination of these might mean you are in an aged-care facility and not a library. It's also a good idea to look for lots of books and to read the sign on the front door.

✰ BE ON TIME:

Any previous battle engagements should be postponed until after the interview. Your advice that you were detained by the Aegean Wars will not be considered favorably. Similarly, your parking problems will not get you any brownie points—they don't really care about the lack of facilities for chariot storage in municipal parking lots. Yeah, sure, they might offer day care, employee health schemes, work bonuses … but what about the really important stuff?

✰ DRESS CONSERVATIVELY:

Leave all your weapons at home. Library administrators are generally disinclined to appreciate the finer points of warfare, even in relation to exit control (and then they wonder why people steal library books!).

Whenever possible, comb your hair before the interview and remove any body parts that were not actually grown by you (e.g., shrunken heads, nose bones, etc.).

If you are going to borrow spectacles, make sure they have glass in the frames. Experienced interviewers are always on the lookout for ways to trip you up.

✰ GIVE YOURSELF THAT EXTRA EDGE!

Refrain from biting, kicking, punching, or other-wise injuring your interviewer, at least until after you've been appointed to the position.

Agree with all personal opinions expressed by the interviewer—regardless of how inane they might be. A word of caution here: Sometimes the interviewer will try to deliberately provoke an inappropriate response. They may also throw in a seemingly casual comment that is meant to elicit a rebuttal from you. Also, sometimes library administrators are just dolts.

If you are having trouble deciding what game the interview is playing, it may be best just to ignore the advice above regarding biting, punching, etc. Just ask yourself first, "Do I really want this job?" before proceeding any further.

Your First Interview

Be polite but assertive.

Part 2 WORKING IN THE LIBRARY

Constitutional Amendments for Library Users

★ AMENDMENT I ★
The Library shall make no law limiting development
of collections relating to religion or controversial issues,
or prohibiting the free access thereof; or abridging the freedom of speech,
except when excessively loud.

★ AMENDMENT II ★
A well regulated system, being necessary to the security of a library, the right
of the people to keep and bear borrowing cards, shall not be infringed.

★ AMENDMENT III ★
No borrower shall, in time of peace be entitled to borrow,
without the consent of the Library, nor in time of war, but
in a manner prescribed by the Library's Policy Manual.

★ AMENDMENT IV ★
The right of people to be secure in their persons, bags, papers, and effects,
against unreasonable searches and seizurres, shall not be violated,
and no warrants shall issue, but upon probable cause,
supported by oath or affirmation, except when the
library' security alarms are triggered.

★ AMENDMENT V ★
No person shall be held to answer for an overdue, or otherwise
malicious damage crime, unless on a presentment or indictment of
the Head Librarian; but shall be compelled in any case to be a witness against
themselves where overdue or damage is concerned.

★ AMENDMENT VI ★
In all disputes, the accused shall enjoy the right to a speedy and public
trial, and to be informed of the nature and cause of the accusation; to be
confronted with the witnesses and documentation against him or her.

★ AMENDMENT VII ★
There is no right of trial by jury; the Head Librarian's decision is final.

★ AMENDMENT VIII ★
Excessive bail shall not be required, nor excessive fines imposed, nor cruel
and unusual punishment inflicted, unless it was really expensive or out-of-print book.

★ AMENDMENT IX ★
The enumeration in these library amendments, of certain
rights, shall not be construed to discourage library use.

★ AMENDMENT X ★
The powers not delegated to the Head Librarian by the Library Board, nor
prohibited by the requirements of the District, are reserved to the employees of
the library, but not to the library users.

Management Models for Library Administration

Cargo Cult Model

Library administration is conducted from a remote location. No one ever sees who is in charge; no one ever knows when funding will arrive or its magnitude. Everyone is very grateful for the fact that something arrives, but they are not sure what to do with it or if it has a specific purpose.

Monolith Model

One person is in charge of everyone and everything. The administrators hardly ever move from their office, and when they do, they expect others to step around them. These people are inflexible in their approach.

Gandhian Model

Based on the philosophy of Mahatma Gandhi, the library administrator listens to everyone's "personal issues," supports proposals for improvement and/or change, and is the office peacemaker. Soft-spoken and philosophical in approach, this person makes management decisions have the **appearance** of being considered in the light of all available data.

Faux-Participative Management

The hallmark of this model is the overwhelming number of committees and committee meetings, generally conducted outside core working hours (i.e., on your own time). Agendas may be formal, informal, obscure, or hidden. The library administrator does not take the chair at meetings, but it is shared in rotation through the committee members. The administrator, regardless of any discussions, proposals, or options that were considered, makes all final management decisions.

more ➔

Dispersed Management

YOU ARE HERE

An organizational diagram shows multiple individuals sharing hierarchical positions. This means that no single person is accountable for disasters, while all can share the accolades for anything that actually does work well. Serves as a retrenchment buffer, but prevents any meaningful change because no real decisions are ever made.

Novocain Model

Administrator needles library staff until work is conducted in a numbed state. Communication is by barely comprehensible mumbling, and everyone is expected to "be brave."

School Library Model

The library staff (often totaling one person) does everything, is accountable to everyone, receives nil recognition for any innovations, and does not appear on any organizational charts.

Management Models for Library Administration

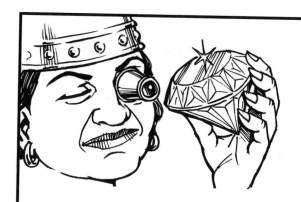

Essential Crystals and Gemstones for You and Your Library

Can you operate your library without ALL of these?

AGATE: All agates enhance other stones.

AGATE, MOSS: Decreases depression, restores mental balance.

AGATE, PICTURE: Sharpens mind.

ALEXANDERITE: Increases self-esteem.

AMBER: Improves decision-making.

AQUAMARINE: Improves expression.

BLOODSTONE: Helps self-actualization, courage.

CHRYSOPHASE: Tranquilizes, sharpens perception.

CORAL: Eases depression, dispels nightmares.

DIAMOND: Eases insecurity.

DIOPSIDE: Relieves insecurity.

EMERALD: Aids working closely with others.

FLUORITE: Increases intuition.

GARNET: Enhances imagination.

HEMATITE: Grounds, protects.

JASPER: Increases endurance, courage.

LAPIS LAZULI: Improves communication.

MALACHITE: Dispels stress, anxiety.

MOONSTONE: Improves intuition and receptivity.

OBSIDIAN: Wards off negativity.

OPAL: Promotes love, joy, and emotional balance.

PEARL: Reduces oversensitivity; peaceful.

PERIDOT: Extends patience.

PYRITE: Dispels anxiety.

RHODOCHROSITE: Strengthens self-identity.

QUARTZ, AMETHYST: Guards against excess.

QUARTZ, CELESTITE: Exudes a calming influence.

QUARTZ, CITRINE: Reinforces self-confidence.

QUARTZ, ROSE: Tranquilizes, calms.

QUARTZ, SMOKY: Balances emotions.

QUARTZ, WHITE: Promotes healing; an energizer.

RUBY: Increases confidence, leadership skills.

SAPPHIRE: Improves communication; mood elevator.

SODALITE: Fosters harmony and communication.

TIGER'S EYE: Balances material and physical needs.

TOPAZ: Relaxes, balances.

TOURMALINE, BLACK: Guards against bad vibes; protective.

TURQUOISE: Heals, offers protection.

... Technology Support Hotline ...

Thank you for contacting the technology Support Group. We care deeply about your well-being and provide this counseling service for those who are anxious about technology, are having difficulty coping with individual aspects of modern life, or just need a sympathetic shoulder to cry on.

We feel your pain—we really do. All of our staff have been through the same traumas and understand your problems. Let us help you on the road to recovery.

Please select from the options below to be connected with an appropriate counselor. If you experience a panic attack during this phase, take three deep breaths and hold the line. An operator will be with you shortly.

Remember—we really do care!

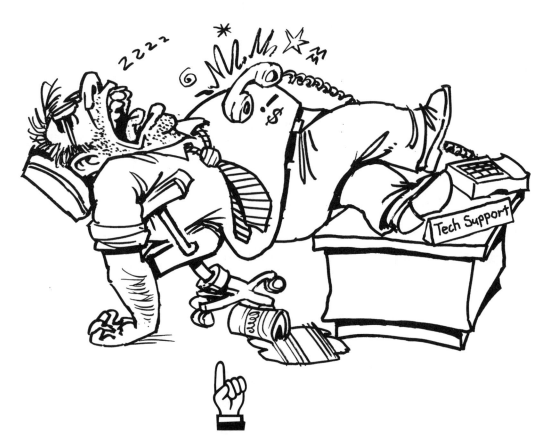

Technical Support
(The Welcome Message)

BLUE SCREEN SYNDROME, PRESS "1"

Ah ... so you are using Windows. Version 3x, 95, 98, NT and ME all produce this effect. There is little we can do for you, I'm sorry to say. You have lost any document that you were working on. You will have to start all over again. Sorry. Close your computer down gently—don't hit it. It's not the hardware's fault. Would you like the name of your nearest Apple agent, or would you like to try Linux?

FREEZE FRUSTRATION FRENZY, PRESS "2"

Ah ... so you are using Windows. Version 3x, 95, 98, NT and ME all produce this effect. There is little we can do for you, I'm sorry to say. You have lost any document that you were working on. You will have to start all over again. Sorry. Close your computer down gently—don't hit it. It's not the hardware's fault. Would you like the name of your nearest Apple agent, or would you like to try Linux?

POST-TRAUMATIC SYSTEMS DISORDER, PRESS "3"

Ah ... so you are using Windows. Version 3x, 95, 98, NT and ME all produce this effect. Close your computer down gently—don't hit it. It's not the hardware's fault. Would you like us to send you a theater guide? Or perhaps a list of recent book reviews ....

DIGITAL DEPRESSION, PRESS "4"

Ah ... so you are using Windows. Version 3x, 95, 98, NT and ME all produce this effect. Close your computer down gently—don't hit it. It's not the hardware's fault. Would you like us to send you a theater guide? Or perhaps a list of recent book reviews ....

NETWORK NARCOLEPSY, PRESS "5"

So, you find your network running so slowly that you are falling asleep? Are you sure that it's not just the tedium of working on something really boring, regardless of how necessary it might be? Follow these steps:
- Get up out of the chair.
- Find a human being to talk with, and forget about it all for five minutes.
- When you come back to your workstation, if you still have not been able to log on to your network, hang up the phone and dial back in.
- Then push either "1" or "2" on you handset [see above]

 The Autotmated Menu

ARIES
March 21 to April 19

The most competitive of all the star signs, these librarians will strive to have the biggest, best, and newest of everything. They attend all conferences, workshops, and symposia for fear that they might miss out on something vital. Worst of all, they will insist on sharing their knowledge with you.

TAURUS
April 20 to May 20

Appreciative of the finer things in life, these librarians tend to be very possessive. Good with reclaiming overdues but will expect a reasonable comfort level at the work site. Dependable and solid. Have a tendency to overeat, so watch length of meal breaks carefully.

GEMINI
May 21 to June 20

Gemini librarians are talkative. Ruled by Mercury, they have a tendency to change their minds frequently, so don't expect books to be in the same place on successive visits to their libraries. They may be responsible for an increase in patron complaints.

CANCER
June 21 to July 22

These are "homebodies" who don't like change. They are also collectors, so they are ideal for culling campaigns. Loyal and faithful, they make good "yes men and women," rarely questioning any decisions. Ideal for promotion to Head Librarian.

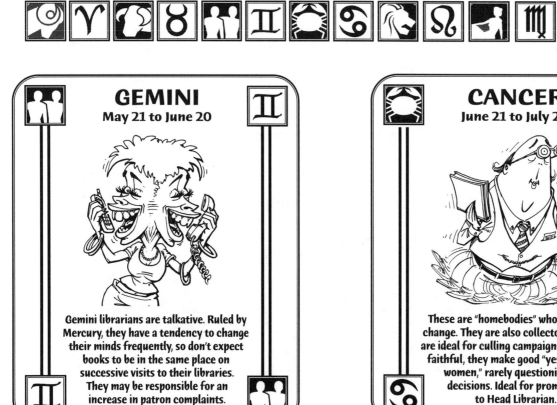

LEO
July 23 to August 22

Leo librarians are born leaders but have a sensitive ego. Don't upset them—they never forget anything. They're given to moping and being surly, so they make ideal reference librarians because usage drops off; this will end up saving you money on this part of the collection.

VIRGO
August 23 to September 22

Fussy to the point of obsession, these librarians are cleanliness freaks. They need routine in their daily lives but hate to impose on others. Sensitive to the environment, with delicate nervous systems. Excel at circulation and morning coffee break organization.

LIBRA
September 23 to October 22

Very bright and social, effective with language, deliberate about practicing social skills and manners, and good at arbitration and diplomacy, these librarians search for win-win solutions that make everyone happy. Look out for your own job—it may be in jeopardy soon.

SCORPIO
October 23 to November 21

Intensity is the name of this sign's game. Everything is a matter of grave importance, or they won't do it. They love to play cat-and-mouse games. Anything where they can go for the kill is fun for them. They make good library administrators.

SAGITTARIUS
November 22 to December 21

Very independent, these librarians enjoy time to themselves. They are likely to close the library at each and every opportunity. Best in archival work away from the public.

CAPRICORN
December 22 to January 19

Diligent, focused, and goal-orientated. In other words, stubborn. Will generate ideas, then delegate the details to others. Not averse to delegating upward, so keep your door shut unless you want to be roped into some real work.

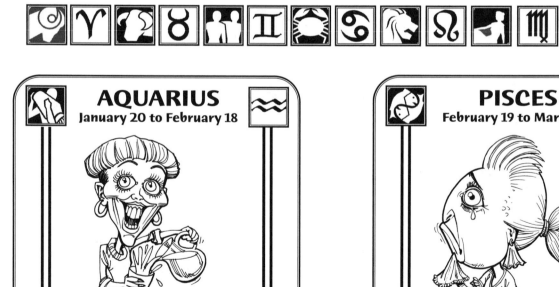

AQUARIUS
January 20 to February 18

These librarians love everything and everyone. They are painful to work with and cause untold stress for administrators. Their tendency to spread cheer and joy is rarely appreciated by coworkers, and library patrons will take advantage of their good nature.

PISCES
February 19 to March 20

The kindest and most caring of all the signs. Rarely able to resist a sob story about lost books. You won't get any work out of them; they'll always be collecting for good causes or acting as grief counselors for patrons, colleagues, or passers-by.

COPYRIGHT WARNINGS

Minimal

Organization/Person ©2003.

Basic

O/P ©2003. All rights reserved.

Standard

O/P ©2003.
No unauthorized copying of this material is permitted without prior permission.

Professional

O/P ©2003.
This material is protected under intellectual property laws. It may not be copied, stored, or circulated in any format, without the express consent of the author.

Psychopath

O/P ©2003.
This is my work. If you even think of using it without my permission, you can expect to have a lot of abusive mail from me. I'll track you down, wherever you are, and bring several of my ugly, large friends with me. I have a medically recognized personality disorder, and the court system is likely to give me lenient treatment if I lose control. So, on second thought, go ahead ... I'm looking forward to it.

Corporate

O/P ©2003.
You may not modify, copy, distribute, transmit, display, perform, reproduce, publish, license, create derivative works from, transfer, or sell any information, software, products, or services obtained from this site.

Any reproduction or redistribution not in accordance with the above is expressly prohibited by law, and may result in severe civil and criminal penalties, is subject to restrictions as set forth in subparagraph (c)(1)(ii) of the Rights in Technical Data and Computer Software clause at DFARS 252.227-7013 or subparagraphs (c)(1) and (2) of the Commercial Computer Software—Restricted Rights at 48 CFR 52.227–19, as applicable. Violators will be prosecuted to the maximum extent possible.

Warrior Librarian

O/P ©2003.
Created by a Warrior Librarian. You have been warned.

Get Great Media Coverage for Your Library Conference with These Publicity Stunts

Grand Opening:
P. T. Barnum was no fool—he knew the value of a few elephants in a street parade. Unfortunately, the availability of pachyderms is severely restricted, but you can always use a few archival photographs on your flyers. PaintShop and similar graphics programs make this really easy. To conform to Truth-in-Advertising requirements, you'll have to get a few larger librarians to dress up, however.

Fireworks:
A really spectacular display would put a significant dent in the conference budget, so time your grand opening to coincide with an event where pyrotechnics are featured. New Year's Eve, Chinese New Year, or any national holiday event is ideal.

Wild Animals:
Always an attention-grabber, utilize public and media fascination with wildlife. These can also be a little expensive to organize, so you can either hold your conference at a zoo or publicize the riotous behavior of librarians following a cocktail party. Maybe just stay with the zoo idea ....

Glue Wrestling:
Forget mud or jelly wrestling—a huge tub of library glue with two scantily clad librarians thrashing around will have the network cameras rolling.

Shelving Trolley Demolition Derby:
The crowd loves thrills and spills, especially if there's any blood involved. Most library trolleys are easily converted into passenger vehicles, so line 'em up, jump on board, and smash away. Any major arterial road is suitable, particularly freeway interchanges.

Wearable Art Fashion Parade:
The Smithsonian Institute is almost certain to purchase your Union Catalog pages caftan trimmed with apricot chiffon or the faux fur–lined borrowing card cape.

Conference Survivor:
Live transmission of conference workshops and lectures. The public gets to "vote off" the most boring speakers, with the last remaining presenter receiving a huge cash prize.

Recipe for Sweet Library with Sauce

INGREDIENTS:

- **One architect**
- **A library board and/or administrator**
- **A selection of carpet samples and paint charts**
- **One library equipment catalog**
- **A fat bank account**
- **A gross of booksellers (tightly bottled)**
- **A low-budget computer consulting company**
- **A handful of trained library professionals**

INSTRUCTIONS:

1. Take the architect and issue clear guidelines as to requirements. The architect will then create a building that bears no resemblance to your specifications. This will be the base of your library.

2. Dip into the fat bank account and line your library base with quality, serviceable carpet. Avoid lime green or dark purple if possible. Spread the sides of your library base with neutral or muted paint. Don't be tempted to use any checkered wallpaper you might have left over from another recipe.

3. In a separate bowl, use your library equipment catalog to select the fixtures and fittings. When you have used all of this budget allocation from the fat bank account, pour the mix into the base. Remember not to fill it right to the top.

4. Dribble a small amount of librarians into the mixture before it starts to set. (Sorry, this should have been Step 1.)

5. Carefully unbottle the booksellers and use very sparingly. When the books become separated from the sellers, use all but one of the remaining librarians to accession, label, cover, and shelve the books. This will consume most of the remainder of the fat library budget.

6. Whip in whatever is left of your fat library budget with the low-budget computer consultants. They will place connection points in the wrong places, so additional wiring will be required later. This will help hold the building together structurally as it ages.

Your library is now ready for consumption. The last of the librarians will provide the sauce for the library. For a really spicy sauce, use a fresh warrior librarian.

The remaining ingredient (library board and/or administrator) should only be used if the library comes out half-baked. You need someone to take the blame.

Using the First Aid Kit in the Library

Sticky Plaster

Not only useful for emergency bookbinding, but also can assist in noise control.

Eye Irrigation

Too much time at a computer screen? Or too many late nights out? Remove the red-eye look. Will not help dark rings under the eyes.

Disposable Gloves

For handling sticky books or other offensive materials.

Cotton Wool

Hearing protection for librarians on rainy days. Also useful for mopping up coffee spills on computer keyboards.

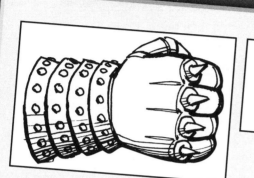

Heavy Duty Gloves

For really nasty things in the library that require handling, make sure you have appropriate equipment.

Thermometer–Non-Rectal Type

Very useful when writing submissions for air conditioning/heating of the library.

Ice

Is always good to have on hand for those very hot days when heat stroke might be a problem.
Also handy for headaches if applied to the cause.

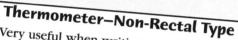

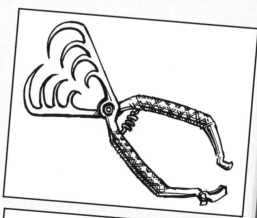

Extractor

For obtaining library fines or payment for lost books, as well as reaching those difficult places under shelving.

As you start your career in librarianship, you will find that you will have to keep your transportation costs to a minimum. But cycling will keep you fit and healthy, as long as you don't breathe in too much smog.

With your first major pay raise, you'll be able to afford motorized transport, although you might have to wait for a while to get the transportation of your dreams.

If you are lucky enough to gain employment in the well-paid, satisfying career of school librarianship, you might be able to save enough before you retire, or burn out, to purchase your own automobile.

TRANSPORT GUIDE FOR LIBRARIANS ⇨⇨⇨

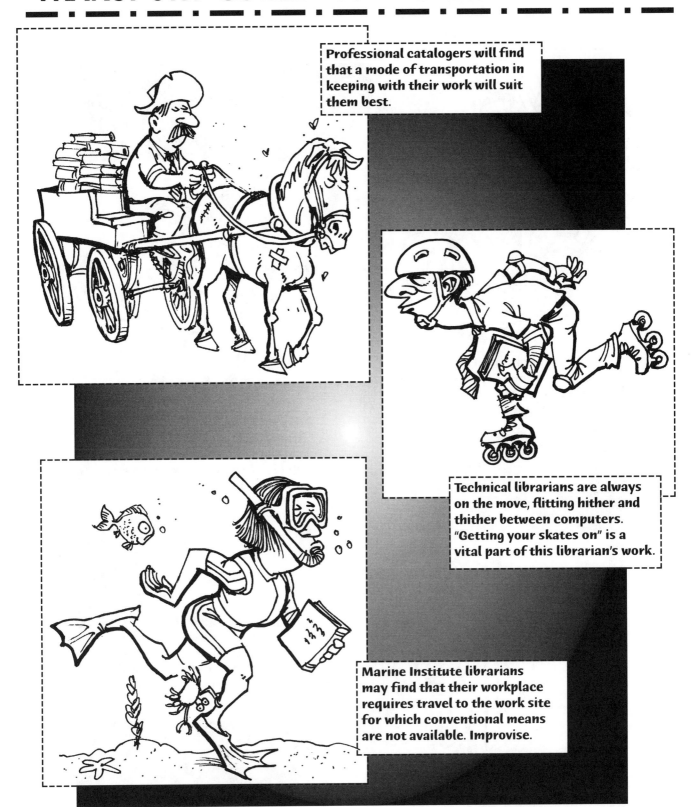

Professional catalogers will find that a mode of transportation in keeping with their work will suit them best.

Technical librarians are always on the move, flitting hither and thither between computers. "Getting your skates on" is a vital part of this librarian's work.

Marine Institute librarians may find that their workplace requires travel to the work site for which conventional means are not available. Improvise.

Rural librarians need all-terrain transportation for providing outreach programs but must select from a range within the library's budget.

Inner-city public librarians need transportation that is easy to park, requires low maintenance, and is a low theft risk. Scooters are ideal because they can be utilized in the workplace.

Art Libraries are often very relaxed regarding the dress codes for their staff. Offbeat forms of transport are common, although you will need to find your own parking space for your equipment.

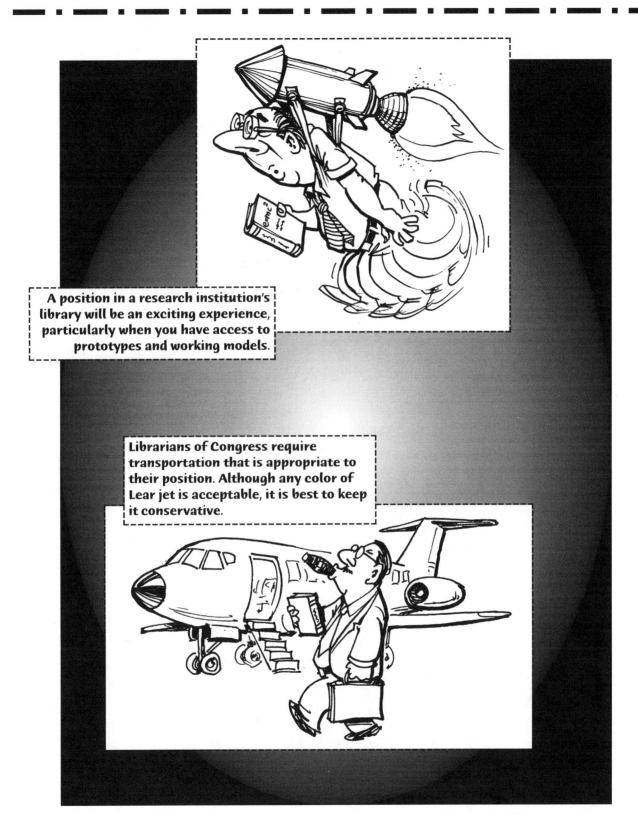

A position in a research institution's library will be an exciting experience, particularly when you have access to prototypes and working models.

Librarians of Congress require transportation that is appropriate to their position. Although any color of Lear jet is acceptable, it is best to keep it conservative.

AND FOR WARRIOR LIBRARIANS ...

Promoting Pulp
The Origin of Blurbs

ORIGINAL REVIEW	EXTRACT FOR BLURB
This book stinks. The author rambles on about nothing in particular; the story lacks any plot or character development. It is so badly written, it doesn't even qualify as *postmodern*. Complete rubbish! Don't waste your time or money reading it—*a masterpiece* in vanity publishing.	*"... postmodern ... a masterpiece ..."*
When I began reading the novel, I found that I couldn't keep my eyes open. It was trite, and quite frankly boring. Highly recommended for insomniacs—there is no medication that can match its effectiveness.	" ... highly recommended ... "
Yet another title trying to capitalize on the recent resurgence of interest in this topic. The author expects you to *indulge yourself* by providing excessive generalization, resulting in an unreadable and inaccurate introduction to an important period of history.	" ... *indulge yourself* ... "
A collection of short stories selected from the works of one of the world's leading writers of complete garbage. Although the author would like one to consider his stories both elegant and whimsical, they are neither.	" ... one of the world's leading writers ... elegant and whimsical ... "
Chronological narrative that starts with the mathematics of the ancient Greeks and finishes with rocket science. In trying to cover *the entire history of scientific achievement* in such minute detail, this work fails in its objective *to engage young readers*. The tiny font is difficult to read, the diagrams and illustrations are of poor quality, and the index provided is minimal. Use this book to press dried flowers—its useless for anything else.	*" ... the entire history of scientific achievement ... to engage young readers ... "*
Lovers of the fantasy genre, or those who are heavily into are trilogies, will be disappointed by these works. A terribly sad imitation of Lord of the Rings. Would have been much improved if the writer had joined the ranks of those whose writing reflects a true understanding the genre.	" ... reflects a true understanding the [fantasy] genre ... "
Complete drivel. *I was very impressed* by the audacity of the author in asking money for this offering. This book has turned me off reading for life. Go to the movies or watch TV instead.	*" ... I was very impressed ... "*

What Librarian is That?
The Pocket Guide to Identifying Librarians

The Duck

While appearing to float serenely, underneath the surface this librarian is paddling like crazy. Placid for most of the time, will hiss and flap when upset, especially when his or her territory is under threat.

The Owl

Nocturnal librarians, specializing in finding resources in dark places. In addition to keen eyesight, they have exceptional hearing and can detect food being consumed in a library from a distance of 100 yards.

The Robin

Highly gregarious, with a complex social order. Flocks remain stable and may contain the same individuals for a number of years. Foraging flocks travel rapidly through bookstores and maintain contact with high-pitched calls.

The Parrot

This noisy librarian is given to mimicking policy-speak and provides a colorful addition to any library. Social habits are generally solitary, mainly due to inflicted isolation.

The Swan

Graceful, majestic librarian, mainly kept for ornamental purposes. A real crowd pleaser at meetings and conferences, this librarian can be depended upon to put on a good show.

The Hawk

These librarians usually hunt with short, silent flights from a perch. They often search for prey during swift flights, surprising their victims and subduing them quickly.

The Eagle

The small beady eyes give the impression of being somewhat sleepy, but this librarian misses nothing. Inhabiting high altitudes, he or she will swoop down to library level silently and pick off prey.

The Rooster

The early riser of the librarian species arrives at work full of news, jokes, and other irritating noise. Noted for its ostentatious display of self-importance.

What Librarian is That?
The Pocket Guide to Identifying Librarians

Occupational Health and Safety

ERGONOMICS:
Make sure your seat is at the right height for your desk if your work involves sitting for any length of time. Luckily, librarians are not required to be sedentary for long periods. Also avoid standing in one position for any protracted time as this will promote the perception that you aren't doing anything important.

LIGHTING:
Recognized standards for lighting will rarely be met in most libraries. Librarians should augment supplied illumination with devices of their choosing. However, you should stay within organizational budget limitations, so be careful with those candles.

RADIATION RISKS:
Computer monitors should be either of the low-radiation type or covered with a radiation shield. Equipment running the Windows system is relatively safe because it is frequently out of service. The greater part of the radiation is generated from the back of the monitor, so try to stay on the screen side. It's also easier to read from that angle.

HAZARDOUS MATERIALS:
Be careful to minimize exposure to fumes from photocopiers, Liquid Paper/White-Out, paints, polishes, many plastics, aerosols, and pest treatments. Be aware of the effects and treatments for corrosive, flammable, or toxic substances. If you look hard enough, you'll find at least 10 reasons why you are unable to attend work on any given day.

ARMED INTRUDERS:
Keep an arsenal of weaponry handy. Most bazookas will fit comfortably under the circulation desk. The common or garden-variety assault rifle is a little too cumbersome to carry while shelving, so leave it under your desk. Ask your regular library supplier for details of their hand gun range.

DISEASE TRANSMISSION:
Despite the urban library myth, viruses are generally not transmitted by contact with books. Bacteria is another matter—always use gloves when handling books and a face mask if working with older books or patrons.

INJURY PREVENTION:
Trip hazards should be removed as soon as they are identified. This includes worn or frayed carpets and smaller patrons. Hot water scalds can be prevented by taking a little extra time and care on your coffee breaks—about 85 minutes is ideal.

AIRBORNE ALLERGENS:
Dust and mould are two of the most potent triggers for allergies. Whenever possible, try to avoid breathing in a library.

FIELD GUIDE TO LIBRARY USERS

Scholaticus Domesticus [Serious Student]

appearance & behavior:
Comes equipped with books, pens, and paper. Doesn't ask for directions or assistance.

habitat:
Nests in quietest part of the library. Often has to be removed at closing time.

Volumen Confectorii [Book Consumer]

appearance & behavior:
Rare. Protected species. Borrows books on a regular basis and returns them before date due, and in an undamaged state.

habitat:
Migrates between new book displays and circulation desk.

Instrumentum Adactio [Equipment User]

appearance & behavior:
Not interested in print resources. Only wants to use computers. Harmless if they suspect they're under observation.

habitat:
Computer areas.

Sonorius
Beastiaria
[Loud Animal]

appearance & behavior:
You can hear them coming, well before they get to the library. Seeks company for converstation purposes only.

habitat:
Will not nest. Sole purpose is to generate noisy disruption.

Parvus
Placidus
[Quiet Mouse]

appearance & behavior:
Very quiet, mouse-like creature. Most of the time you won't know they are there.

habitat:
Generally nest in reading area, reading.

Furunculus
Serpens
[Sneaky Snake]

appearance & behavior:
Smiling, friendly, appears very sincere. Always has a cheery greeting for library staff. Predator. Causes disruptions to nests of other library users, plus damage to equipment and resources.

habitat: Found in all library areas.

Wait! There's More! ▶

FIELD GUIDE TO LIBRARY USERS

Innocuus Nomas
[Harmless Nomad]

appearance & behavior:
Vacant expression, hands in pockets, often doing a "silent whistle." Wanders in, wanders around, wonders why, wanders out.
habitat:
Not confined to any single area of library.

Alternus Bibliothecii
[Visiting Librarians]

appearance & behavior:
Often indistinguishable from ordinary library users. Notable behaviour includes spontaneous shelfsorting, OPAC familiarity, and competent handling of large books.
habitat:
Generally in reference, fiction, or nonfiction. May request access to special collections.

Bellator Bibliothecii
[Warrior Librarian]

appearance & behavior:
Similar in behavior to *Alternus Bibliothecii*, but look for subtle differences in appearance.
habitat:
Everywhere.

55

Alternative Library Designs

THE BUDGET MODEL is for administrators who like to do more with less. This open-plan library suits outdoor settings and has natural lighting, timber uprights, and an adjustable shade awning.

THE ENERGY SAVER will cut your power bills with a tried and true Dutch design that's fully self-sufficient on windy days. Patrons are advised to duck their heads on entering.

TROPICAL HUT is the perfect choice for sunny beachside locations. Made from low-cost building materials, it comes with piped Hawaiian music and optional grass skirts for the librarians.

THE BUCKMINSTER FULLOFBOOKS

is ideal for the scientifically minded. Pit your intellect against this technological puzzle as you figure out how to place square shelves in a round building.

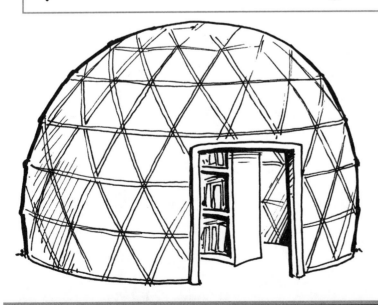

Alternative Library Designs

BARGIRL STYLE is perfect for attracting male patrons, especially in red-light districts. Administrators should be advised that a liquor licence is needed, not to mention female librarians require some dancing experience.

FAIRYTALE DESIGN is the ultimate children-friendly library. It comes with an elderly lady with vast experience in nursery care. (The charges against her for child neglect were never proven.)

HIGH SECURITY
offers maximum protection for your literary investments, with its sturdy construction that not only keeps villains out but also keeps your librarians in, especially when fitted with a time lock.

THE EARLY MODEL
is a stock clearance item. A back-to-basics library for more primitive administrators who still haven't evolved beyond stone tablets. Comes with a cavernous storage space and is suitable for librarians limited to grunting patrons.

THE CAMPING SPECIAL is a mobile library with a difference. Administrators can relate to it because it has a thin skin, gets in a flap, and is forever changing its position.

STREETWISE is the latest in cheap libraries for cities with high mobile populations. It features flow-through ventilation, a place to throw empty wine bottles, and is made from fully recycled materials.

NORTHERN EXPOSURE is the latest cool design. It comes with an arched weatherproof doorway and thick seals on the windows. Unsuitable for warm climates as stock can get liquidated.

THE BUREAUCRATIC RUNAROUND caters to ambitious librarians, without anyone feeling left behind. Also prevents any challenge to library administrators, who may prefer to climb a corporate ladder.

Children's Collections

BLOW YOUR MIND!

NOISE WORKS

All the latest drumkits

Break the sound barrier in your bedroom! We'll show you how...

Tap shoe Revues

NOISEWORKS: A bimonthly magazine for younger readers. Offers reviews on high-volume toys and a do-it-yourself feature for creating sounds that push the limits of human endurance.

Children's Collections

PRECOCIOUS

Are you a genius?

TRY OUR MENSA TEST INSIDE

Swell Your Head

All the latest wunderkind goss
How to be **a rocket scientist**

PRECOCIOUS: For children who love to show off to adults who don't have their own children. Features stories, games, and activities for 5- to 10-year-olds. Each issue offers practical information and ideas for driving people crazy.

Young Adult Collections

TART MONTHLY: The journal for modern misses who like to look cheap. Packed with information on bad makeup and recycled clothing, this magazine serves as a guide to contemporary fashion for teenagers who like to meet "interesting" people.

Young Adult Collections

SERIOUSLY ANNOYING: Is edited for girls ages 12 to 19 and features the latest trends in creating tension at home and school. Read about what parents really hate and how to get grounded for the rest of your life.

Literary

OBSCURE

How to Cultivate
an Air of Pretension

Latest
Art
Reviews
~but do
you care?

Make sure nobody understands you
by acting French

OBSCURE: Those interested in the fashion trends of the literati
will learn the latest color preferences for berets, how to swagger
in an overcoat on a hot day, and how to cultivate just the right
length of facial hair. Look like a writer without the hard work.

Education

UPHILL Battlers' Guide

Will Your Students Make the Grade?

Are you over the hill as a teacher?

UPHILL: A journal for professional educators to ease them through a day at work. Total psychological support, stress management, and black-line masters to keep students busy and quiet so you can do the crosswords or have a nap.

EXHAUSTED: For parents who prefer to home tutor their children, this publication presents helpful tips and advice. Read how to get the groceries during field trips, how to cook family meals and pass it off as Home Skills lessons, laundry as a method to meet mandatory science outcomes.

Travel

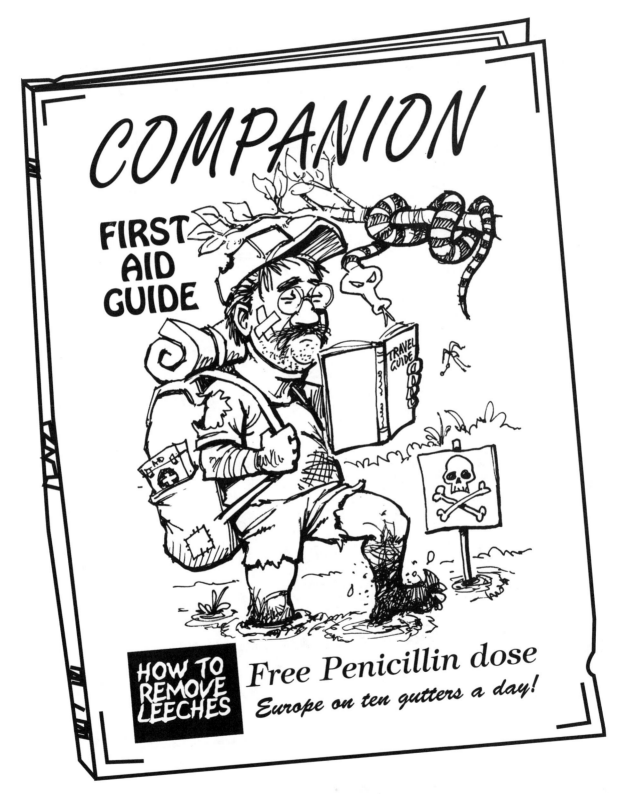

COMPANION: Is written for the active, adventurous traveler. Why give in to the challenge of jet lag, local water contamination, or lost reservations? Features tear-out postcards to keep in touch with those at home.

BAGGAGE: Your personal guide to where your luggage might be sent. Whether near or far, the team from BAGGAGE has been there, but their personal effects probably didn't make it. Useful foreign phrases for intimidating disinterested airline clerks.

LIFESTYLE

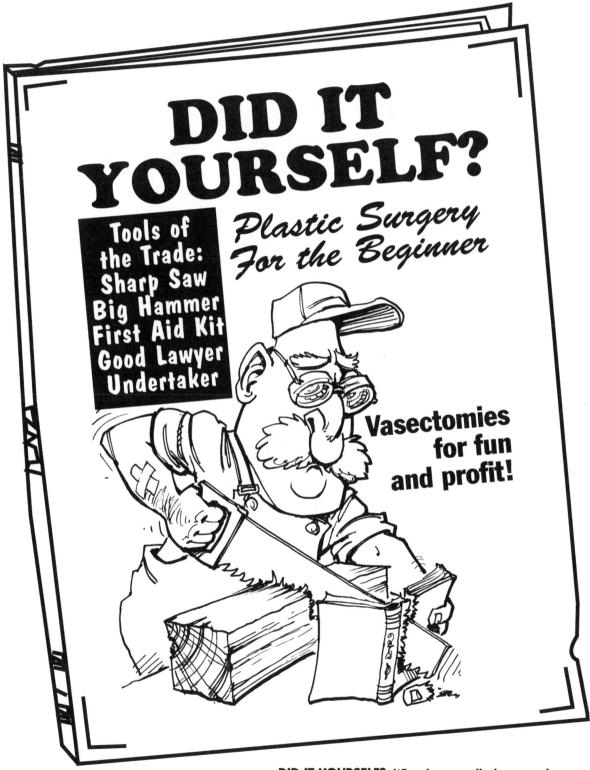

DID-IT-YOURSELF?: Who do you call when your home project collapses on passing strangers, or where do you get that one vital missing screw for the self-assembled furniture item? Includes hilarious letters submitted by readers currently involved in expensive, protracted legal action—as either plaintiff or defendant.

FOGEY: The extremely elderly are encouraged to be proactive in avoiding family commitments, feuds, and visits. Who wants to baby-sit the grandkids at your age? Read suggested answering machine messages that won't cause alarm (but will discourage visits) and research into walking assistance aids and incontinence as a conversation starter.

Medical Conditions for Sick Leave Forms
(They'll Never Ask for the Details!)

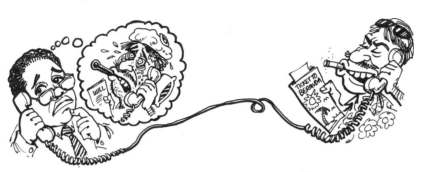

Aegrotatia: Just sick—and didn't want to go into the details in writing.

Acidius Vulnia: Paper cut on finger—didn't want to bleed on the books.

Suspected Alopecia Areata: Hair loss—found some loose hairs on my comb, thought I'd better rest for a day or two so I didn't drop hair into the computers.

Capillary Hemangioma: Birthmark—needed to get some natural light on it, so I went to the beach.

Ceterumia Negotium: Other occupation—worked at second job to help supplement meager librarian's salary.

Concisus Amoria: Broken love—broke up with boyfriend/girlfriend, too embarrassed to go to work because librarians aren't supposed to have a love life.

Dolensic Decollia: Painful head, otherwise known as a hangover.

Epidermal Ephelides: Freckles—didn't want to get any more sun exposure by going outside, so spent the day watching cable TV.

Inopia Celeritatis: Chronic lateness—just running later than usual, but I came the next day.

Invistic Potissimus: Disagreement with the administrator—couldn't stand the thought of seeing him/her.

Impedimentum Memoriae: Faulty memory—couldn't remember where I worked.

Osteoignavus: Bone lazy—didn't feel like getting out of bed.

Papula Maxima: Big pimple—too embarrassed to go to work because this was my day to be at the circulation desk.

Seborrhea: Dandruff—stayed home and washed hair in case it was contagious.

Trichotillomimima: Pulling out hair—working in the library is driving me crazy!

REFERENCE DESK

Form #101: Request for Assistance

1. What information are you looking for?

2. What information should you be looking for?

3. Where have you already looked?

4. Where should you have looked?

5. Why didn't you look there first, before coming here?

6. How many times have you used the library in the last month?

7. How many times should you have used the library in the last month?

8. How urgent is your information request?

9. If it was that urgent, why didn't you ask sooner? (25 word limit)

: Special Interest Groups :

GOVERNMENT AGENCY PROTOCOLS (GAP)

This group is mainly composed of computer nerds with knowledge of government accounting procedures. They will transfer small amounts of money from multiple government accounts into a Swiss bank. This will fund an annual junket to somewhere really nice for tired, stressed, or burned-out librarians, thereby helping to address the inequities between the librarians' salary and their true value.

SPECIAL COLLECTIONS ABOUT MIRTH (SCAM)

As working in a library is no laughing matter, it is important that the librarians maintain morale—both their own and those of their staff (if they are lucky enough to have any). Therefore, this special interest group will scour the face of the earth—or at least publishers—for books on library humor. They will be given paid time off from work, an expense account, and unlimited time to ensure that all librarians have something to laugh about. The resultant special collection will be accessible to all librarians ... if the SCAMmers ever come back.

RESOURCE AND INFORMATION SHARING KNOWLEDGE-WORKERS (RISK)

To reduce professional embarrassment, without further undue expenditure of skinny library budgets, librarians will be able to transfer resources between libraries—this will fill gaps in collections and create a surplus at stocktake. This special interest group will coordinate the stocktake times so that no one shows a loss.

LIBRARIANS EAGER TO GET WELL ABOVE XML (LEGWAX)

Electronic publishing frontiers are always pushing the boundaries of reasonable learning curves. Just as we master HTML, XML rears its ugly head. With web-based subject support from libraries rapidly augmenting the print collection, librarians are just going to have to develop their own mark-up language, which should be developed in conjunction with the catalogers of the Library of Congress. Being entirely incomprehensible to anyone but librarians, we'd be Internet gods!

there's more...

: Special Interest Groups :

TEACHING OF TERRIBLE STUDENTS (TOTS)

Every library has a hard core of younger patrons whose sole purpose for existing is to make the librarian's life sheer hell. This special interest group will investigate legal, practical means either to get these kids to conform to reasonable standards or to change districts—if not planets.

DISTANCE-LEARNING ONLINE HELP (DOH)

In recognition of the need to support remote learners, this special interest group will construct websites, issue print guides, travel vast distances to present workshops, give up holiday time, and produce audiovisual material to ensure that students studying by remote mode are able to plug their computer into a power socket before pushing the "on" button.

RURAL OR REMOTE TECHNICALITIES (RORT)

Building on the principle that fear is a powerful motivator, librarians in areas classified as either rural or remote will publish details of the discomforts, disasters, and ding-a-lings that they endure. Snakes in libraries, evacuations for fire/flood/plague, waiting for three months for a computer repair, and the like are suitable topics. The group will coordinate publication and ensure national news coverage at least in the gutter press. Politicians, fearing an outcry from the populous, will immediately boost funds for these libraries. (Like, yeah ... right ....)

Beauty Tips from Linda Absher, The Lipstick Librarian

Love those new pastel, retro eye shadows but can't afford the new millennium price tag? Mix 'n' match using a rainbow assortment of highlighters! They come in those dazzling '60s shades! (WARNING: Some colors can stain permanently.)

No time for a tan? Lean your face within three inches of a computer monitor for at least 30 minutes for that quick, back-from-Brasilia glow! (Also great for warming up leftovers!)

Get rid of that nasty shiny-nose problem using books that haven't been checked out since the Nixon administration. Simply flip the pages back and forth in front of your face for that sophisticated (though gray) matte finish. (Not to be attempted by those with asthma or dust allergies.)

Tired of answering those routine reference questions like "where's the bathroom?" Writing those answers on old conference badges then pinning them on strategic parts of your body saves hours of effort and frustration.

Tattooing all your round-table and association acronyms on your body is not only one of the hottest library fashion trends, it's also handy when you need to list your memberships on those pesky conference or grant applications.

Forgot to put on mascara this morning? Paint small Post-it notes black, cut into fringes, and stick onto eyelids for that Liza Minelli/*Cabaret* look!

Plastic bands that wrap around Xerox paper cartons make nifty conference badge or eyeglass frame holders.

Feeling a little peaked in the afternoons? Give yourself a refreshing blast from one of those pressurized air cans used for dusting computer keyboards. (WARNING: Do not confuse with WD-40 or clown air-horns.)

Make a sleek (albeit weighty) carrying case with matching jewelry from all those demo computer disks and CD-ROMs from vendors. String together with magnetic strips and Velcro binding.

Wadding the perforated-hole strips from the sides of computer printout paper makes for an excellent exfoliating body scrubber.

Catalogers' Secret: Cornhusk lotion makes a fast-acting facial mask as well as a wallpaper stripper and thickening agent for soups and stews.

Want to perk up story time when telling The Hobbit? Make chain-mail clothing out of paper clips!

Snag those padded envelopes from ILL—the rag paper/lint stuffing makes a wonderful mud pack!

See the Lipstick Librarian's website at http://www.lipsticklibrarian.com/

Library Desiderata

Go placidly amid the noise and haste,
and remember what peace there may be in silence.
Whenever possible, without surrender,
ask patrons to keep the noise down.

Speak your truth quietly and clearly;
and listen to others,
even to the dull and ignorant;
sometimes they're good for a laugh later.

Avoid loud and aggressive persons;
They are vexations to the spirit,
and may be in a position to have your budget cut.

If you compare yourself with patrons,
you may become vain or bitter,
for always there will be greater
and lesser persons than yourself;
even though some real doozies
will come through the door.

Enjoy your achievements as well as your plans.
Keep interested in your own library, however humble;
jobs are scarce, and it's paying the rent.

Exercise caution in your business affairs,
for the world is full of trickery.
But let this not bind you to the same booksellers;
many persons strive for high turnover,
and everywhere life is full of bargains.

Be yourself. Especially do not feign knowledge.
Neither be cynical about research;
for in the face of all innovation and progress,
it is as perennial as the grass.

Take kindly the counsel of your support group,
but don't let anyone else pull your strings.
Nurture strength of spirit to shield you in tricky cataloging.
But do not distress yourself with dark imaginings.
Many phobias start with library glue and spine labels.

Beyond a wholesome diet,
treat yourself to chocolate occasionally.

You are a graduate of library school,
though less appreciated than you deserve;
you are paid to be here.
And whether or not it is clear to you,
no doubt AACR2 is comprehensible to some.

Therefore be at peace with God,
whatever you conceive Him to be.
And whatever your labors and aspirations,
in the noisy confusion of the library,
have peace in your meal breaks.

With all its sham, drudgery and broken books,
it is still a beautiful library.

Be cheerful.

One day you might inherit a lot of money.

Thin Books for Busy Librarians

COLLECTION DEVELOPMENT

- Government White Papers for Children to Enjoy
- Sex Education Books That Won't Offend **Anyone**
- Math Fiction For Young Adults
- Quality Reference Materials for Under $10
- Technology Titles with Long-Term Currency

LIBRARY MANAGEMENT

- Accessing Digital Resources Without Computers
- Budget Submissions That Are Guaranteed to Work
- Common Sense Library Design in Action
- Copyright-Compliant Methods of Website Preservation
- Feng Shui for Library Workrooms
- ISO Standards and Guidelines for Paper Clips
- Using Correspondence Students as Library Monitors: A Practical Guide

LIBRARY OPERATIONS

- Acceptable Expletives to Use at the Circulation Desk
- Black-Line Masters for Date Due Slips
- Cataloging for Fun and Profit
- Location Options for Spine Labels
- Using Shockwave for Authority File Maintenance

BIBLIOGRAPHIC INSTRUCTION

- Case Studies: Successful Introduction of Beowulf to Reluctant Readers
- Library Lessons That Became Blockbuster Movies

LIFESTYLE

- Color-Coordinating Your Wardrobe to Match the Library Carpet
- Comfortable, Yet Stylish, Shoes for Library Ladies
- Fantastic Holidays on a Librarian's Salary
- The Collectors' Guide to Wooden Catalog Card Boxes
- Tips for Keeping Your Love Affair Secret from Other Library Staff
- How to Achieve Peace and Harmony at a Busy Circulation Desk

PROFESSIONAL DEVELOPMENT

- Conference Proceedings: The Shelving Initiative
- The General Public's Concerns in Respect to Library Management Issues
- Index of Libraries in Antarctica
- Successful Self-Promotion for the Timid Librarian
- The Wit and Humor of Library Administrators

2001: A Library Odyssey:
The onboard computer flying the library has a personality defect. Can the library staff get to the manual override and keep circulation functioning?

A Few Good Librarians:
Tom Cruise takes on the cause of school librarians in a court battle when they are falsely accused of not doing much except stamping books and shooshing people. He wins.

Cataloger:
Russell Crowe goes to library school, gets a job in a library, and finds himself chained to the processing department. His library administrator forces him to cover books, make spine labels, and maintain authority files; he hopes to win his freedom, but dies.

Ernest Goes to the Library:
Dimwitted Ernest finds that the library has books that you can borrow for free, so he joins a reading group.

Home Alone 8:
A small boy becomes separated from his parents. He goes to the library, where he reads until his parents come to collect him.

In the Company of Librarians:
Tom Berringer stars as a retired librarian who comes back to help in a staffing shortage at the local library.

Indiana Jones and the Temple of Tomes:
Harrison Ford battles assorted bad guys, snakes, and booby traps to fight his way into a library so that he can get first pick of the new acquisitions.

Library of the Apes:
This movie depicts a futuristic school library where the budget is controlled by simians dressed as humans.

National Lampoon's Animal Library:
College students infest the campus library, vomit, damage books, and leave gum under tables. So, what's new?

Overdue Notices of the Third Kind:
Richard Dreyfus glimpses the possibilities of other life forms when he repeatedly defaults on his book returns.

Patch Atkinson:
A children's librarian, played by Robin Williams, brightens up the somber atmosphere in the library and shows kids how much fun reading is.

Rambo: First Overdue Notice 2:
Sylvester Stallone reacts (or is that "acts"?) badly to a request for the return of his overdue books.

The Blair Library Project:
Innovative film techniques (i.e., poor-quality cinematography) show how scary it is to work in a library.

What Librarians Want:
Mel Gibson stars as a library administrator who finds that he can read librarians' thoughts. He takes early retirement.

Fictitious Filmography
(Movies for Librarians)

PUBLISHERS' REWRITE REQUESTS

Where many great works of literature were created in a fit of pique after the original manuscript was abruptly returned with a terse note ....

.... FROM THE EDITOR ....

Dear Ms Rowling,

We received your draft manuscript entitled "The Demise of Fantasy in Children's Literature." We will not be publishing this work because our research shows that children are still enjoying stories about witches and wizards. Perhaps you'd like to look into this facet of literature before you submit further manuscripts?

TO: Thor Heyerdahl

RE: Submission of "Luxury Cruises of the Pacific"

Sir, you may not be aware that there has been a significant move away from overly indulgent holidays. You're pretty much up the creek without a paddle, as it were.

PUBLISHERS' REWRITE REQUEST

Dear Margaret Atwood,

We thought your submission "Strengthening Family Bonds" has some merit, but you need to include some recognition of increasing trend toward dysfunctionality in families.

MEMO

MEMO TO EDITORIAL STAFF:

This J. R. R. Tolkien idiot has sent another thick parcel. This time its called "Organizational Behavior in Academic Institutions." Can someone in your department let him know that he's not going to get anywhere if he keeps making his characters sound like strange creatures running around in the woods? And tell him to cut back on the wordage. Much too descriptive.

Thanks.

Dr Robert C. Atkins,

Thanks for your book on chocolate cookery. We have tried out many of your recipes and have to say we've all gained a few pounds. However, there are already too many books on this topic.

FROM THE PUBLISHER

Edgar Allan Poe:

Sir, your "Tour of Medieval Castles" is not a publishable work. The general public has no interest in pointless rambles through boring old buildings.

Bob,

Enclosed is a proposal for a book called "A Detailed History of Time" by Stephen Hawking. I think that if he provides enough depth and detail, we might have something here for the school kids. What do you think? Can you get back to him on this?

A NOTE TO THE AUTHOR

Dear Dr. Benjamin Spock,

We are unable to consider your work "Contraception Made Simple" as it does not acknowledge the precepts of the national campaign to encourage compassionate child-rearing.

To: Charles M. Schulz

There are already many publications in print on the topic of your thesis, "Peer Group Pressure and Its Effects on Education." We would, however, be interested in something a little lighter in approach that would have appeal to a wider audience.

Hi, Douglas Adams,

"Astro-Tourism: The Potential for Cost-Effective Space Travel" is a very predictable treatment of the future possibilities of what we here laughingly call "galactic adventures." Have you ever considered writing humorous science fiction?

Footbook:

The Action Sport for Librarians

NATIONAL FOOTBOOK PLAYOFFS
(Terminology Explained)

Automatic Shift :	Librarians take part in a roster of duties, at different times of the day
Balanced Lineout:	An equal number of patrons and librarians exit the building
Button Hook:	To grab someone by the shirt and tear off a clothing fastener
Center Snap:	The librarian on duty suddenly loses his or her "cool"
Cornerback:	Area of the library where rubbish accumulates
Dead Ball:	Soft, spongy sphere (used to relieve stress), now squashed flat
Down and In:	Suffering depression but still going to work anyway
Extra Point:	To do a favor for the library administrator
Free Agent:	Unemployed librarian available for work on any team
Fly Pattern:	Dirty black marks left on a clean surface
Free Kick:	To take advantage of someone's error
Full Back:	To return to duty after a meal or other break
Fumble:	To have someone see you drop a book (no witness, no fumble)
Half Back:	To commence returning from a break and then to change your mind
Hash Marks:	Greasy smears left on books read at fast food outlets
Interference:	Movement that prevents library work from happening efficiently
Line of Scrimmage:	Queue at circulation desk five minutes before closing time
Multiple Offense:	Set of salary scales for information professionals
Overtime:	Hours at work beyond normal rostered shifts, generally unpaid
Penalty Kick:	To enjoy discomfort of patron having to pay library fine
Punt:	To take a chance, for example on a story about an overdue book
Quarterback Sneak:	To go to a meal break and to reappear briefly before disappearing again
Running Back:	To overstay approved length of time for a break and then having to rush
Straight Arm:	To defend oneself by being as brutal as possible to the attacker
Three-Point Stance:	To present a case using a trio of arguments
Touchback:	To provide a tactile cue to support a library eviction
Wide Out:	Library exit of extra width for wheel chairs, strollers, or large patrons

TRAVELING LIBRARIANS
Never Far From A Book

International Travel
"Must Visit" Sights for Librarians

INDIA: The National Library, Calcutta

Their pamphlet display is overwhelming, given that everything is reproduced in all 15 of the nation's recognized languages. The reading room is located 5 km away from the main building, which ensures patrons get the right book the first time. However, this is not as inconvenient as using the family records collection for India—it's located in London, England.

ITALY: Vatican Library, Rome

Popes have always had libraries, and not being limited by an acquisitions budget, were able to buy just about anything they wanted. Don't expect exhibitions to be restricted to religion-related realia; you'll also be able to gawk at Henry XVIII's love letters. Now there's somebody who knew how to avoid alimony payments.

USA: Library of Congress, Washington, D.C.

The largest library in the world, this contains more than 120 million items housed on approximately 530 miles of shelving. The library receives more than 22,000 items per day and adds approximately 10,000 to the collection. You should see ITS backlog!

UNITED KINGDOM: Bodleian Library, Oxford

The original artwork for the cover of Tolkien's *The Hobbit* is on display, as are the usual librarianalia. What makes this library particularly special is its shopping arcade, the proceeds of which help support the library: mousepads for around $60, paperweights about $130, not to mention the Shakespeare high ball glasses. Somehow, it's hard to imagine the Venerable Bard on the cocktail circuit.

SWEDEN: Royal Library, Stockholm

Umlauts abound, but there is little evidence of pine furnishings. The permanent exhibition of Swedish posters is not what you might think. Also on display are the recent antiquarian acquisitions, but who wants to look at a bunch of old people?

CHINA: The National Library, Beijing

Significant Buddhist texts and many other ancient documents. Worthy of souveniring here is the list of rules for library users, who are (among other things) forbidden to scribble, asked to keep flammable products in lockers provided, and required to dress neatly. For those of us used to seeing the word "juvenile" followed by the word "offender," the Children's Services Division offers many alternative paradigms of youth programs for libraries.

GERMANY: Humboldt University, Berlin

A number of libraries exist on the campus, but of cultural interest is the extent to which book burning was conducted under the Nazi regime. Students were authorized to carry out the torchings, and the librarians are still trying to recover fines for book destruction. So far, Interpol, Mossad, and the FBI have not located any of those responsible for violating the library's Responsible Library Use Policy.

AUSTRALIA: National Library, Canberra

Purchase kangaroo and koala toys from the gift shop, the main foyer, the reading room, the inquiry counter, the restaurant, the taxi stand, and both the male and female rest rooms. hard to imagine the Venerable Bard on the cocktail circuit.

Writer's Workshops

One of the world's most famous horror writers presents a workshop on the genre and shares the secrets of his phenomenal success. Bring pen and paper, a cushion, a silver stake, and a crucifix. Budding writers with heart conditions are advised to select another workshop session.

Workshop—STEVEN KING

To be held at 48 Doughty Street. Entrance via back lane, through hole in fence. Wear old clothes and bring some orphans. If you have any really tragic personal experiences, be prepared to share them with the group.

Workshop—CHARLES DICKENS

She sits in the darkened room, breathing heavily and thinking of the past. The smell of roses fills the air, but she remembers another type of perfume. Dark. Powerful. Magnetic. Only money has that scent. Will she reveal the secrets of churning out romance novels? An adventure not to be missed.

Workshop—BARBARA CARTLAND

Got a scientific theory you'd like to prove? Learn the secrets of generating controversy, successfully dealing with peer rejection, and getting a best-seller published.

Workshop—CHARLES DARWIN

with a Difference

Author of *Mein Kampf* and former European dictator discusses the process leading him from a career as a house decorator into politics, and thence into the field of literary endeavor.

Workshop—ADOLF HITLER

Examine the popular appeal of short books providing pithy advice. Bring red felt-tipped pen and red cardboard. Ties not required, but please keep your shirt collars buttoned.

Workshop—MAO TSE-TUNG

Be amazed, astonished, astounded, dumbfounded, and flabbergasted at the process of putting a thesaurus together. Hands-on activities to absorb, distract, engross, animate, enliven, quicken, beguile, charm, delight, enchant, and fascinate the budding wordsmith.

**Workshop—
DR. PETER ROGET**

Take a behind-the-scenes look at the methodology in constructing both 1 : a reference book containing words usually alphabetically arranged along with information about their forms, pronunciations, functions, etymologies, meanings, and syntactical and idiomatic uses; and 2 : a reference book listing alphabetically terms or names important to a particular subject or activity, along with discussion of their meanings and applications.

**Workshop—
NOAH WEBSTER**

The author responsible for creating the best-selling book ever in the history of publishing.

Workshop—GOD

Haute Couture for Librarians

The Academic Librarian
Dress to impress by emulating the wardrobe of faculty members, especially those faculty who determine the budget allocation. A tweed jacket with open-neck white shirt, caramel slacks, and brown loafers will serve well for both practical wear and fashion requirements.

ENGLISH ACCESSORY →

The Legal Librarian
Dress for success in Brooks Brothers' outerwear. Ivy League ties are always impressive with quality suits. Although dressing this way will stretch your meager salary to the maximum, you'll find that your employers will be less likely to expect you to do the hack work in the library, and you'll be able to make a better case for clerical assistance.

Silvertail District Librarians
Dress with finesse to provide wealthy library patrons with a sense of confidence. However, pearls and beehive hair should be restricted to female librarians.

Inner Suburban Public Librarian
Dress for access by creating empathy with library patrons. If you work in a tough neighborhood, you'll find facial piercing and tattoos will complement your grunge hairstyle and matching wardrobe. If nothing else, you'll blend in with the crowd in the event of a riot.

Research Librarians
Dress in excess if your workplace supports a hazardous industry. Your employer should provide you with appropriate protective clothing. The standard hazmat suits, breathing apparatus, and safety equipment are also suitable for school librarians to counter the standard conditions found in many government schools.

Librarians in Religious Libraries
Dress to transgress librarianship stereotypes by being excessively conservative. Basic black garments with a splash of white around the neck will blend in well, with your need to express your individualism being subtlety expressed by your accessories. May also be suitable for school librarians in educational institutions administered by religious groups.

Defense Library Workers
Dress to coalesce in jungle fatigues, which are not only comfortable to wear, but also show your employer that you are a "team player." Appropriate armory also deters petty theft and unauthorized removal of resources. Also suitable for school librarians in inner-city schools.

Resort Librarians
Dress to repress any barriers between you and your patrons. Many upmarket resorts now offer library facilities for the use of their guests. Be guided by the theme of the resort, be it tropical, adventure, or nudist. Not suitable for school librarians.

THE WARRIOR LIBRARIAN QUIZ

When presented with a sob story about lost books, do you:

1. Believe the patron without question? (0 points)

2. Consider the possibilities of truth, and then politely ask for payment? (1 point)

3. Refuse to consider the story, then threateningly demand payment? (2 points)

4. Hold up score cards for originality of story, and then wipe out an appropriate percentage of the library fine? (10 points)

Your budget has just been cut, again. Do you:

1. Quietly accept economic rationalism? (0 points)

2. Offer suggestions for fund-raising? (1 point)

3. Threaten to resign if there are any additional cuts? (2 points)

4. Nod and smile, then plot the down-fall of the administrator responsible? (15 points)

You get passed over for promotion in favor of a complete dolt with half your intelligence and none of your qualifications. Do you:

1. Accept this without question? (0 points)

2. Enroll yourself in yet another course in order to gain further qualifications? (1 point)

3. Buy the appointee a kitten or puppy as a congratulatory present? (5 points)

4. Bonus 20 points if you know they are allergic to pet hair.

You win an incredibly large amount of money. Do you:

1. Put it away for your retirement? (0 points)

2. Give some to charity, spend some, and invest the rest? (1 point)

3. Take early retirement and inform your ex-boss of your opinion of him/her and his/her management of the library? (5 points)

4. Stupidly keep working and bequeath the whole lot to a library? (subtract 10 points)

SCORE CARD

0–10 points: You are an incredibly nice person, but you have yet to master the finer points of Warrior Librarianship. If you don't do something about this, and soon, you are doomed forever to Drabdom.

11–20 points: There are still vestiges of remnant decency about you, although you are well on your way out of the Doormat Stakes.

21–30 points: Whoa! Chances are your colleagues, patrons, and administrators don't mess with you too much. Just some work needed in some areas.

Over 30 points: Congratulations. You are already a Warrior Librarian. Either that, or your math needs further development.

The Language of Book Gifts

What Do They Reveal?

 ROMANCE: It would be nice to think that you are viewed as a romantic, but the sad truth is that if you get a romance novel as a gift, you are viewed as an airhead with nothing much to occupy your time.

 HUMOR: No, you are not considered to be witty. The present-giver wants you to become an amusing conversationalist, but thinks you are dull and boring at the moment.

 THRILLER: You are seen as leading a cloistered life, and someone wants you to have a little vicarious excitement in your life.

 EARLY CHILDHOOD: If you are female, and not pregnant, lose some weight fast. If you are male and unattached (and like it that way)—run!

 GARDENING, COOKING, OR CRAFT-MAKING: This is a present from an insecure cheapskate who knows that flowers or chocolates are ephemeral. Rather than having to give you another gift in the short term so they stay at the forefront, you get an oversized book you can't ignore.

 DICTIONARY: Perhaps you "um" and "ah" a lot? The gift of a dictionary means someone is interested in what you have to say but wants you to say it better.

 ATLAS: Receiving an atlas means you need to broaden your horizons. A street directory, however, indicates you just need to get out more.

 WITCHCRAFT: You really don't need to be told, do you?

 GIFT CERTIFICATE: This is not an indication that the giver is lazy, is ignorant, or doesn't know you very well. You are viewed as being independent and able to select books for yourself.

Yoga for Librarians

SMALL PATRON EXTENSION

Practice this position for communicating with young library users.

SEEK AND FIND

Locate small objects (paper clips, thumbtacks, earrings) that may have fallen behind you on the floor. Particularly good for fragile or sharp objects you don't want to walk on.

LIBRARIAN LIFT

Placing boxes on high shelves in store rooms usually means a ladder is required, but by practicing this position, a librarian is able to balance another librarian to reach those difficult places where there isn't room for a ladder.

THE TALL STRETCH

Useful for exercising those muscles most used in reaching books on high shelves and for offering thanks for surviving another day in the library.

HUMAN SIGN

Answer patrons' directional queries by forming the human sign. Not only will this help the hearing impaired, it will deter patrons from returning to repeat the same stupid question.

EXIT CONTROL

Imagine your security system alarms have just been activated … what posture is appropriate for librarians? Repeated practice of this position will result in arm extensions and will maximize your coverage of doorways.

ORGANIZATION CHART

Demonstrate your place in the library hierarchy by indicating your position (at floor level) and your administrator (in the clouds).

VERMIN EVASION

Where unpleasant microfauna inhabit your library, don't lose valuable time jumping up on chairs. This exercise will stop things crawling up your legs while you work at your desk, although you might need a cordless keyboard and mouse.

1446 B.C.: Moses checks out two clay tablets from Mt. Sinai but is charged replacement costs by librarian Tess T. Ment because they are found to be waterlogged and smoke damaged and have maps of Egyptian deserts scribbled on the back.

1000 B.C.: King Solomon achieved fame as a sage and poet. He was credited with extraordinary wisdom and became a legendary figure in Judaism. However, it was his librarian Sy Tasion who provided him with statistical reports and summaries with which Solomon then made his now-famous judgments.

Little Known Librarians of Antiquity

400 B.C.: Confucius became famous as a sage in China and ultimately influenced the civilizations of all of eastern Asia. It is not widely known that a quiet woman named Fi Ling cataloged his scrolls and maintained the archives of his library. Without these technical services, there would be no "Eastern Philosophy."

300 B.C.: Although Plato's philosophic reputation is well known, his many hours of research at the Athens Municipal Library were logged by the reference librarian, Iess Bien. It remains a matter of record that on no less than six occasions, Plato was spoken to regarding his failure to leave at candles out.

200 B.C.: Hannibal's huge army crossed the Alps with the help of Ellie Phant, the readers' guidance librarian at Carthage Central Library. At least 6 pachyderms were loaded with high-interest, low-reading-level resources to keep the 40,000 soldiers entertained on the cold nights and on rest days.

A.D. 64: Sue Donim, operations librarian at the Rome Memorial Library, repeatedly applied for additional fire extinguishers. Unfortunately, Nero's accountant had slashed the library budget that year, and the rest is history.

Little Known Librarians of Antiquity

A.D. 450: Attila the Hun was able to maintain his interest in children's literature through remote document delivery. Barb Arian (librarian at the National Library of Scythia) forwarded journal article reprints to Attila as he moved around conquering countries and slaying people.

A.D. 880: King Alfred the Great was a regular patron of the Saxon Central Library. Popular myth has it that he was beaten up by a housewife for allowing cakes to burn as he slept after a major battle. A letter from Maggy Zine (circulation manager of Saxon Central) dated two days after the event states that Alfred was actually reading at the time of his culinary negligence. It can happen to anybody.

Naturopathy for Librarians

BENEFITS

Make a soothing, relaxing infusion of the following ingredients, and you'll feel much better! These unscientifically proven herbal remedies will improve your eyesight, hearing, ability to think, skin, immune system, digestion, energy levels, breathing, stress and anxiety, and borrowing rates.

RECIPE

Use a pinch of each of the dry ingredients and a cup of each of the liquids:

Aloe Vera	Pcynogenols	Blockers	Yohimbe
Eucalyptus Oil	OPC's	Valium	Dioscorea
Cointreau	Whiskey	Co-Enzyme	Magnesium
Pancreatin	Cayenne	Q-10	Tequila
Arginine	Glucosamine	Ouzo	Valerian Root
Gin	Saw Palmetto	Kava Kava	DHEA
Folic Acid	Chitosan	Used Barcodes	Magnesium
Protein	Ginkgo Biloba	St. John's Wort	Calcium
Supplement	Selenium	Colloidal	Vanadium
Beta Carotene	Chondroitin	Silver L-	Dong Quai
Germanium	Sulfate	Glutamine	Melatonin
Pleurisy Root	Brandy	Super Green	Bourbon
Calcium	Hawthorne	Algae	Vitamin B-12
Vodka	Berry	Mead	Echinacea
Ginseng	Rum	Colloidal	MSM
Psyllium	Shark Liver	Minerals	Vitamin C
Soluble Fiber	Oil Library	Cider	Eyebright
Cat's Claw	Paste	L-Tyrosine	Herb Niacin
Disprin	Chromium	Wild Yam	
Vitamin A	Iron	Copper	
Gota Kola	Starch	Lecithin	

METHODS OF APPLICATION

Drink as a tea or in a cocktail glass with a wedge of lemon; rub on skin, inhale as vapors, or tip over troublesome library patrons.

LIBRARY PARLOR GAMES

PASS THE BUCK

Requires two or more players. One of the usual library dramas (e.g., missing item, security breach, end-processing omission) occurs. The object is to progressively apportion blame so that the guilty party does not ultimately cop the blame.

CHARADES

For one patron and two or more library staff. Lighten the day by selecting a patron at random who requests assistance. Librarian 1 gives clear, competent instructions, then librarian 2 steps in to give conflicting information. If further librarians are available, then they join in with more information that contradicts all previous information. All librarians playing then argue among themselves. Volume must progressively escalate until either the patron leaves or the administrator arrives.

RORSCHACH SHADOWS

This is a variation on the "Shadows on the Wall" game. Librarians use the photocopier on the darkest setting, and copy body parts. This creates black smudgy images, which the other players then have to identify, thus revealing their personality defects.

FRUIT BOB

Using one large pineapple in a bucket of water, invite colleagues to try to pick it out of the bucket with their hands behind their back. For variations, try heavy small fruit (e.g., plums) or add something unpleasant to the water. The object of this game is to keep talkative colleagues at bay so you can get on with your work.

HIDE THE EQUIPMENT

Select one unique piece of equipment that is vital to library operation and hide it. All players then search for the missing item until it is either found, they give up, the library closes, or you get fired.

HOBBY GUIDE

PINTUCKING

PINTUCKING is a relaxing pastime where you can use your love of precision to make attractive decorations for the walls of your library. You might like to use a particular theme, such as "Library Patrons."

MOUNTAINEERING

MOUNTAINEERING improves physical fitness as well as providing spectacular views. If working in the library is making you climb the walls anyway, perhaps this hobby will combine your natural inclinations with an activity you can continue during your leisure hours.

AEROPLANE MODELLING

AIRPLANE MODELING is ideal for those librarians with a fascination for flight and a surfeit of paperwork. Combine these two facets to create an interest you can share with colleagues, patrons, and administrators.

INCOMING MAIL

PASTE

OCCULT STUDIES

OCCULT STUDIES are not only fascinating, but you can also put many of the ancient skills to practical use in your library. Try your hand at voodoo. Even if it doesn't actually achieve the desired results, it's a great way to relieve stress.

ADMINI-STRATOR

MIRCO AQUASPORTS

MICRO-AQUASPORTS are an adaptation of the outdoor variety. Where budget or time is limited, librarians may find this hobby ideal when you want to "get away from it all," but you only get a 30-minute lunch break.

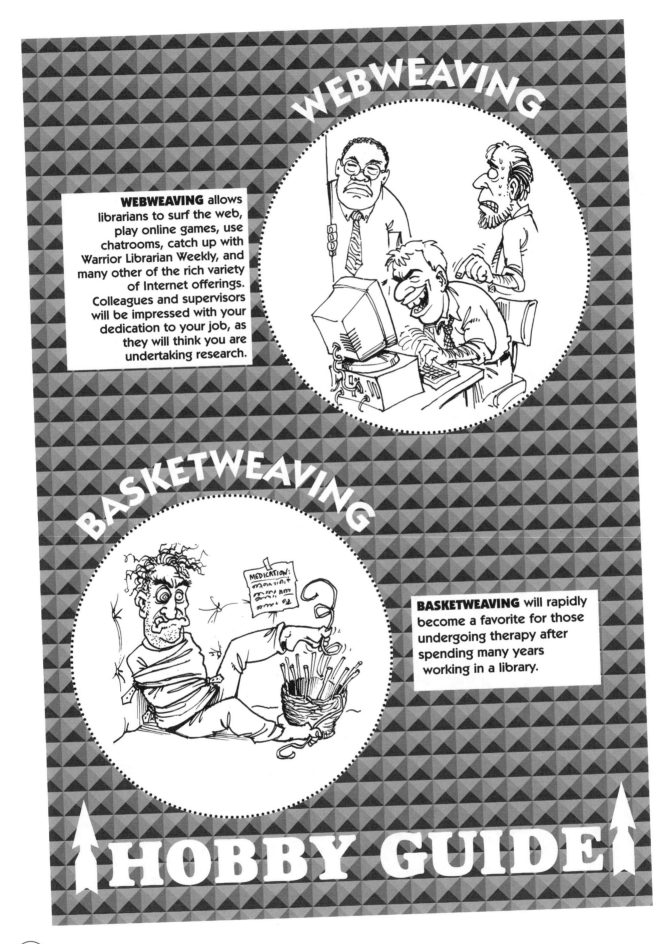

WEBWEAVING

WEBWEAVING allows librarians to surf the web, play online games, use chatrooms, catch up with Warrior Librarian Weekly, and many other of the rich variety of Internet offerings. Colleagues and supervisors will be impressed with your dedication to your job, as they will think you are undertaking research.

BASKETWEAVING

BASKETWEAVING will rapidly become a favorite for those undergoing therapy after spending many years working in a library.

HOBBY GUIDE

Hallmock Library Greetings

From the Library

For Our Favorite Patron
Roses are red,
Violets are blue;
We're sorry you're sick,
But your book's overdue.

Good Luck in Your New Career
This parting gift speeds you on your way,
To a better job, with double the pay.

Greetings to Our New Library Administrator
Welcome to our happy band,
Of librarians bold and brave;
You'll last much longer here if you,
Remember we're not robot, servant, or slave.

Just to Say Thank You
I wish there were a better way,
To express my heartfelt thanks;
For your use of MY hard work,
That allowed YOU to climb the ranks.

On Your Upcoming Birth
We wish you well as you start to glow,
We thought it was just the Big Macs;
Now we know what you were doing there,
All those times up behind the stacks.

Corporate Season's Greetings
Your local library wishes you well,
As this year comes to an end;
Don't forget to borrow lots of books,
To reverse the circulation trend.

For Our Colleague
Your shelving, it is peerless,
Your catalog's just neat—
We only wish you'd do something,
About the smell of your feet.

On Your Retirement
You've served our library well, old friend,
And now we can tell you true;
You've given us lots of laughs for years,
'Though the butt of the jokes was you.

Happy Birthday
We wanted to get you something nice,
But you know what our pay is like;
So please accept this worn-out old book,
And join us next time we go on strike.

Sympathy On Your Loss
Pack up the sack cloth and the ashes,
Your sorrow you must unhook;
We've all lost friends at some time,
But remember—it was only a book.

To Do List: Write These Books

HARRY POTTER AND THE RESEARCH ASSIGNMENT (Contact J. K. Rowling): Harry and Hermione undertake a library project. No magical shortcuts, just a lot of hard slog.

THE EMPEROR'S NEW LIBRARY (Contact Hans Christian Andersen): The librarian is alone in showing there is actually no library, just a lot of mouldy old books.

UNBELIEVABLE! LIBRARIANSHIP AS A CAREER STEP TO THE STATE SENATE (Contact Paul Jennings): Exploring the fantastic opportunities for advancement

NOT FAR ENOUGH FROM THE MADDNING CROWD (Contact Thomas Hardy): Tragic story depicting the sole librarian's attempt to have a 5-minute break.

NONSENSE AND INSENSIBILITY (Contact Jane Austen): Period-style piece on librarians' working conditions.

MEDIOCRE EXPECTATIONS (Contact Charles Dickens): Stretching the library budget to the maximum, collection development becomes a treasure hunt for bargains, second-hand books, and donations.

THE LIBRARY AT POOH CORNER (Contact A. A. Milne): Christopher Robin, Tigger and all of the gang try to build a library in a rotten tree trunk.

A CHAT WITH THE BAT (Contact Dr. Seuss): A rhyming story of a typical Reference Interview, told from the perspective of a younger patron.

ALICE'S ADVENTURES IN LIBRARYLAND (Contact Lewis Carroll): Alice follows the promise of a substantial budget to a new library, then meets Tweedledum and Tweedledee of the Library Board.

LIBRARY OMERTA (Contact Mario Puzo): Thriller based on a librarian's struggle to break the "code of silence" of colleagues and encourage participation in pro-active advocacy.

LORD OF THE FILES (Contact William Golding): Savagery erupts when the decision is made to no longer maintain Vertical (Pamphlet) Files.

STACK (Contact James A. Michener): Thoroughly researched, thick tome detailing the evolution of libraries, cast of thousands.

TINKER, TAYLOR, SOLDIER, LIBRARIAN (Contact John Le Carré): Thriller, traces the subversive nature of librarians across four continents.

THAT (Contact Stephen King): Supernatural tale of pictures and articles disappearing from periodicals; chairs left awry; mysterious phone calls from booksellers.

THE MISSING MONOGRAPH (Contact Agatha Christie): Mystery, of the who-borrowed-it-last variety.

JURASSIC LIBRARY (Contact Michael Crichton): Horror story of library books from past ages being repaired and recirculated. Copyright violations and plagiarism run rampant.

THE FRENCH LIETENANT's LIBRARIAN (Contact John Fowles): Romantic story concerning the importance of good researching skills in providing essential information to the military.

A BRIEF HISTORY OF GRIME: FROM CLEAN SHELVES TO USED CHEWING GUM (Contact S.W. Hawking): Largely incomprehensible discussion on how quickly libraries become dishevelled in the course of a single day. One for theorists and academics

101 LIBRARIANS (Contact Dodie Smith): Disney Studios will want the screen rights to this hilarious story of mirth and mayhem at a library conference.

JONATHON LIVINGSTONE LIBRARIAN (Contact Richard Bach): Fairly pointless animal story; needs a terrific music score for the film version.

BETTER HOMES AND LIBRARIES (Contact a panel of Interior Decorators): How to tart up a dark, drab library with folk art on computers and some cleverly draped fabric.

LIBRARIANS ARE FROM MARS PATRONS ARE FROM VENUS (Cowritten with John Gray): Humorous story on the differences in perspective. Maybe not so funny?

WHERE THE WILD THINGS AREN'T (Contact Maurice Sendak): Mini-book on library listserves.

First There Was the Disney Channel, then the History Channel, and now...

THE LIBRARY CHANNEL
PROGRAM GUIDE FOR TODAY

6:30 A.M.: Librarian Rage
(Reality) Savagery, slander, and innuendo, with a nice cappuccino. (PG)

7:30 A.M.: Biography: Melvil Dewey
(Historical) Profile of the genius, which is as full of contradictions as the man himself. Quietly unassuming a renowned cataloger; was he a gloomy failure at romance? (PG)

8:30 A.M.: The Wrath of God: Cataloging
(True Story) Beneath a library's scenic façade lies one of nature's most damning furies. (PG)

9:30 A.M.: Crown & Country: London's Libraries—Whitehall to Buckingham
(Educational) Where are the photocopiers? (G)

10:00 A.M.: Ancient Mysteries: Miraculous Libraries of Venice
(Historical) Of all the world's greatest cities, none defies nature and logic like Venice. This jewel of the western civilization, built on the water, stands bravely against time and tide, weathering the floods that have threatened its existence. How do they stop the books from getting moldy? (PG)

11:00 A.M.: History's Greatest Blunders: Battle of the Bulge
(Lifestyle) Is the twentieth century the only century in which librarians battled with their waistline? (PG)

11:30 A.M.: Modern Marvels: Salt Mines
(True Story) Why is it your turn to shelve?

12:30 P.M.: Biography: Biblia
(Historical) Profile of the genius, which is as full of contradictions as the woman herself. She dresses like a pauper—because of librarian's salaries. A renowned web designer; is she a gloomy failure at romance? (PG)

1:30 P.M.: In Search of History: Theater of Blood
(Historical) In 1642, British theater was wiped off the face of the Earth. Were librarians to blame? (PG)

2.30 P.M.: Information Science: Library Conferences
(Documentary) If only the general public knew what really goes on, there'd be no stereotyping. (PG)

3:30 P.M.: Biography: Lipstick Librarians
(Historical) Profile of geniuses, full of contradictions; are they failures at romance? (PG)

4:30 P.M.: The Grand Tour: Africa—The Grand Safari
(Travel) Explores the mystique of the ancient continent: Africa, throughout the ages, and the wealthy men of Europe and America who traveled there in search of realia. (PG)

5:30 P.M.: Crown & Country: Libraries
(Educational) Presents an insider's guide to England, featuring famous landmarks such as the National Library. Narrated by Prince Edward of Wessex. (G)

6:00 P.M.: Secrets of the Aztec Empire
(Historical) In the 1970s, workers digging a ditch in Mexico City unearthed a stone decorated in relief—that discovery led to bigger finds, including the Great Library of Tenochtitlán. Join archaeologists as they shed new light on the Aztecs, who grew from a wandering band called the Mexica to the dominating force of pre-Columbian Mexico. (PG)

7:00 P.M.: History's Greatest Blunders: The Bay of Pigs
(Historical) What is safe to eat from a conference's buffet table? (PG)

7:30 P.M.: In Search of History: Asteroids
(Historical) Asteroids have been colliding with the Earth since the beginning of time. The effect can be enormous—from the killing of the dinosaurs to scarring of the planet's surface. Through computer recreations and interviews with the world's foremost asteroid authorities, we explore the history of these rocks from space and future threats to libraries that they pose. Disaster recovery of the greatest magnitude. (PG)

8:30 P.M.: Biography: Che Guevara
(Historical) Looks at the controversial life of the Argentinean revolutionary who was not only a medical doctor but also an aide to Fidel Castro in the Cuban Revolution and active in leftist guerrilla movements in the Congo and Latin America. In 1967, while leading a guerilla action in Bolivia, he was captured and executed, without his library books being recovered.

9:30 P.M.: The Windsors: I'll Be Damned if I'm a Fine Defaulter
(Historical) On the eve of the First World War, King George V changed the family name to Windsor to escape overdue fines. (G)

10:30 P.M.: Librarians Rebel: On Our Way?
Are we ready for contact lenses? Which hair styles are non-bunnish? Dare to be different without resorting to Lycra! (PG)

11:30 P.M.: Biography: President Bush
(Biography) The man might be a fine leader for contemporary America, but what do we know about his borrowing record? His reading habits? How effectively does he use information?

12:30 A.M.: The Grand Tour: New Zealand
(Travel) Explores the mystique of this island country: Are there really libraries for sheep? (PG)

1:30 A.M.: Crown & Country: Buckingham Palace WCs
(Educational) Presents an insiders' guide to royal ablution facilities. What reading material is provided for visitors? Narrated by Prince Edward of Wessex. (G)

2:00 A.M.: Secrets of the Wombat Empire
(Historical) In the 1960s, workers digging a ditch near Brisbane unearthed a chewed rock—that discovery led to a new theory on the marsupial's poor eyesight. Join paleontologists as they shed new light on Australian macrofauna and their ancient attempt to subvert library administration for their own evil gains. (PG)

3:00 A.M.: Movie Time: The Mummy
(Entertainment) See a female librarian portrayed in a movie as a strong, intelligent, and attractive adventurer. (PG)

5:30 A.M.: Movie 2: The Mummy Returns
(Entertainment) See a librarian portrayed in a movie as a wife and mother, who is also intelligent, attractive, strong, and adventurous. (PG)

Companion Animals for Librarians

Skunks
are terribly misunderstood, are underappreciated, and have suffered bad press for generations. They are only offensive when threatened and make an ideal companion for library administrators, who share many of the same attributes.

Pet Rocks
are great for the less mobile librarian. They are low-maintenance friends that don't require feeding, walking, or daily care. You won't have to find homes for their offspring and they also make useful doorstops or paperweights.

Owls
are ideal for busy librarians who arrive home exhausted and collapse on the couch for a few hours before being able to eat their evening meal. You will find the nocturnal habits of their feathered friends a comfort in the small hours of the morning when you can't sleep.

Companion Animals for Librarians

Frogs

are jovial little creatures who take up little space. Their soothing croaking will create a tranquil effect, and they will eat many of the insects that inhabit a library. A little squashy, however, if trodden on.

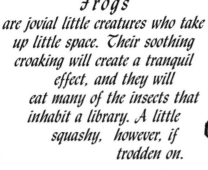

Snakes

are quiet animals requiring little maintenance beyond feeding and housing. For librarians who enjoy mounting exhibits of precious or rare documents, the addition of your cuddly friend to the showcase will be a security bonus for your library.

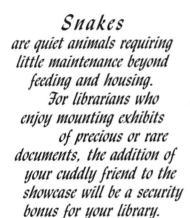

Marsupials

Never have enough room in your handbag or pockets? These pouched friends can provide that little extra space for your library keys, makeup, laptop computer, or any other of life's necessities.

Companion Animals for WARRIOR Librarians

Rabbits
can be litter-trained, are soft and furry, and make little noise. Although they can also be aggressive, less than 10 people per year die from rabbit attacks.

Fish
come in a great variety of colors, sizes, and types. Not only are they delicious baked, grilled, or broiled, they are the low-fat, high-protein alternative to the usual. Juveniles can be kept in a glass bowl until they reach eating size.

Pigs
are not nearly as messy as depicted in popular literature. They are highly intelligent, trainable, and have clean toilet habits when provided with the right amenities. They also don't smell as bad as some library patrons you're likely to meet.

Companion Animals for WARRIOR Librarians

Butterflies
are not especially sociable animals, but they are quiet, make little mess, and rarely bite. Their short life span makes them ideal for librarians who don't want a long-term commitment.

Hedgehogs
are well-behaved animals with multiple benefits. They are great paper spikes and will ensure that no one sits in your seat when you leave it unattended.

Ants
can be free-ranging or contained in "ant farms." Either way, they are much more interesting than most television programs. These pets have the added advantage of being great little tricksters when they get into your colleague's lunch.

ANT FARM

Companion Animals for WARRIOR Librarians

Termites

An upgrade from the common ant, these industrious little insects are an inspiration to all librarians. Observe them removing obstacles from their path, and watch how they make themselves comfortable regardless of any policies, procedures, or previous practices.

Cats

Curl up with a good book with kitty purring away on your lap. As smaller cats can be an irritating trip hazard, it is recommended that Warrior Librarians select from the larger breeds.

Bears

Although Warrior Librarians may have outgrown the teddy bears of their childhood, they will find that something soft and cuddly will continue to be a great comfort in times of stress.

Companion Animals for WARRIOR Librarians

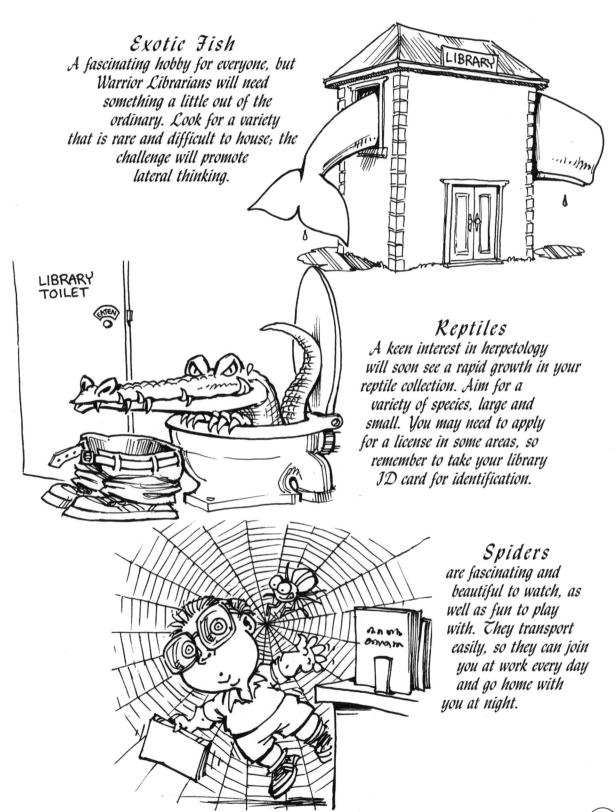

Exotic Fish
A fascinating hobby for everyone, but Warrior Librarians will need something a little out of the ordinary. Look for a variety that is rare and difficult to house; the challenge will promote lateral thinking.

LIBRARY

LIBRARY TOILET

EATEN

Reptiles
A keen interest in herpetology will soon see a rapid growth in your reptile collection. Aim for a variety of species, large and small. You may need to apply for a license in some areas, so remember to take your library ID card for identification.

Spiders
are fascinating and beautiful to watch, as well as fun to play with. They transport easily, so they can join you at work every day and go home with you at night.

Librarians' Fractured Fantasies

Wouldn't a fairy godmother be great for the library? She'd be able to change library vermin into additional staff and rotting food scraps into new book trolleys. Sadly, all these benefits would have a time limitation and at midnight would change back to the same scabby stuff you had before.

Get rid of the old cow (every library has one), and send Jack to the markets. He would supply seeds for magic beanstalks that reach up to the giant's treasure box, which would help with many financial difficulties. Unfortunately, lighting in the average library is so bad that there is no chance of any plants growing to maturity.

A goose that lays golden eggs would negate the need for budget submissions, allocations, or finance reports. You could just go out and get everything that you need, want, or have seen in other libraries. But have you seen the mess that geese make? Someone will have to clean That up. Makes used gum seem pleasant by comparison.

A genie, whether bottled or free range, would be perfect in any library. Not only could you have any resource that you wanted, you wouldn't need to worry about who is going to process and shelve all those new materials. As long as it wasn't Barbara Eden—she'd make everything worse, and that wouldn't be at all funny ....

Put out the welcome signs for Santa Claus! He will cheerfully listen to all your requests, and maybe even give you some candy. Unfortunately, you'll only see him in December. Even worse, you'll still have to wait for your parents to get you that new 16-CD stacker, the new edition of The Complete Oxford with all 24 volumes, or a state-of-the-art computer laboratory.

The Swiss Library Knife

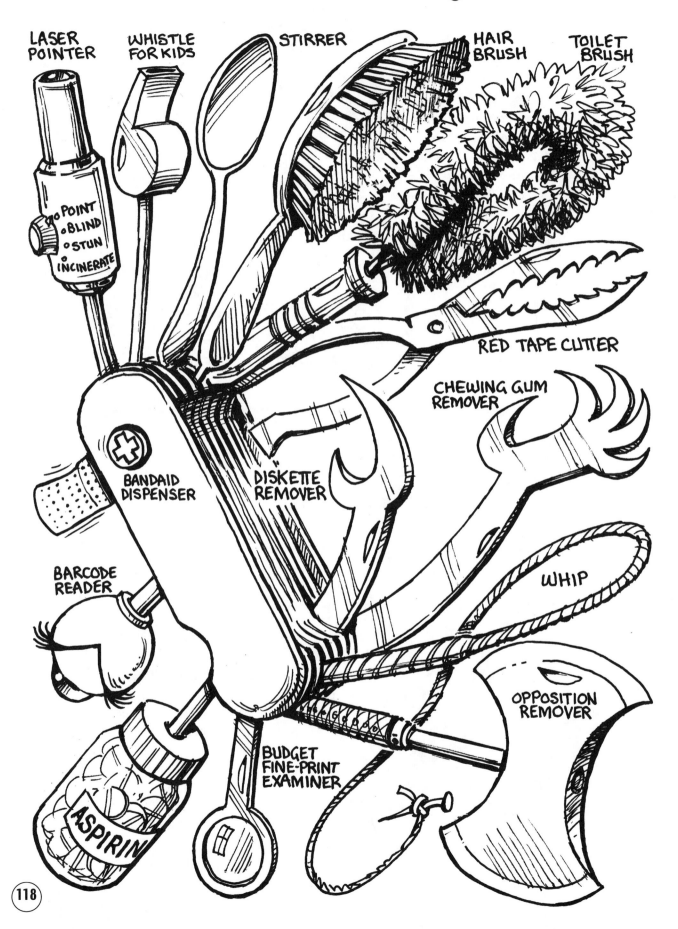

Part 4 THE ULTIMATE CHALLENGE: SCHOOL LIBRARIANSHIP

'I TAUGHT THEM EVERYTHING THEY KNOW!'

Installing a New School Librarian

School Librarians V2003™

OPERATING INSTRUCTIONS

CONGRATULATIONS! You have been very fortunate in obtaining this genuine information professional. If used with care, and in accordance with these operating instructions, your new School Librarian V2003™ will give many years of exemplary service. Improper use or neglect will void your warranty on School Librarian V2003™.

UNPACKING Your new School Librarian V2003™ has left our care packaged with the latest technological skills, an awareness of current issues, managerial techniques to maintain your current school library (while continuing development and upgrading), the ability to contribute to teaching and learning, and a high level of commitment to the application of best practice.

> **!** Please do not discard this wrapping. In addition to providing buffering in transport this packaging is necessary for the operation of your new School Librarian V2003™. **!**

OPERATING INSTRUCTIONS This unit is designed to function within a normal range of temperature and humidity conditions. Excessive heat, cold, or moisture will prevent optimum operation.

Place School Librarian V2003™ in a position that allows maximum visibility. Although the unit will function as a "stand-alone," maximum benefits are gained from networking to other school personnel.

The unit will automatically generate input into multiple areas of school operation. While the feedback provided by the unit may be ignored, this may prove detrimental to the educational output of the school.

PLUG-INS School Librarian V2003™ has been equipped to operate with minimal support. It is recommended that you consider the following third-party additions for maximum enhancement of the quality of your school library programs:

- Administrative Commitment 2003™
- Budget Allocation 2003™
- Professional Development 2003™
- Clerical Support 2003™
- Flexible Scheduling 2003™

KNOWN ISSUES Please ensure that School Librarian V2003™ does not come into contact with School Board Circa 1960 because conflict will arise.

School Librarian V2003™ is not compatible with either Classroom Teacher Circa 1970 or School Principal Circa 1940 to Circa 1980. Upgrades are available for both Classroom Teacher and School Principal in print journals or Internet downloads, although installation of these upgrades may prove difficult. School Librarian V2003™ can undertake these upgrades, but this will slow down operating speeds in core functions.

WARRANTY

WARNING! NEVER overload your School Librarian V2003™. This will result in burnout and will void this warranty. As many satisfied customers have noticed, the School Librarian V2003™ is capable of exemplary operation in many areas outside its core functions. Although very robust, School Librarian V2003™ is, after all, only human.

Important Safeguards for Using Your School Librarian

Save These Instructions

Before using your new School Librarian, it is important that you read and follow the instructions in this Use and Care Booklet, even if you feel that you are quite familiar with this type of employee.

For Your Safety

When using school librarians, in order to reduce the risk of fire, electric shock, and/or injury to persons, basic safety precautions should always be observed, including the following:

• To protect against various types of damage, do not immerse the School Librarian in water or any other liquids.

• This person is not intended for use by the mentally incapacitated, the pedagogically challenged, or without appropriate supervision. Never leave any member of school staff (without sufficient training) in charge of your school librarian.

• Young children do not need any supervision when playing with this person. The School Librarian provides all necessary supervision.

• Ensure the School Librarian is allowed to be turned off when not on duty. Although he/she will frequently reengage outside school core hours, it is important to make sure that the School Librarian has time to reflect.

• Do not operate the School Librarian with an inferior policy or practice.

• Do not attempt to repair or disassemble the School Librarian. There are no user-serviceable parts.

• Do not place any part of this School Librarian on or near a hot gas or electric burner.

• To avoid an overloaded circuit, do not operate another high-wattage person in the same area.

• Do not use outdoors, except by request.

Before First Use

When using the School Librarian for the first time, test out on a small class to ensure that the goods work as described. The School Librarian may smoke slightly when used for the first time; this is normal and will soon cease.

Note: Consistent with our continuing product-development policy, improvements may have been made that render the contents of this package slightly different to that shown on the packaging.

5 Top Tips for School Librarians

1. Never allow visitors to your library to upstage you. You will lose credibility and respect and ultimately, therefore, control over your patrons.

2. Be prepared for any emergency. Keep a large stock of candy, Band-Aids, and tissues handy at all times. This will cover just about any disaster that can befall a school library.

3. Give yourself permission to do crazy things. The kids are going to make fun of you anyway. Because "possession is nine-tenths of the law," act as if you're possessed, and you get to make up your own laws. No one argues with crazy people.

4. Always expect the unexpected. This will occur at the least convenient time and in the most inopportune way possible.

5. Don't expect teaching colleagues to understand the importance or nature of your work. Keep a large file of documents for them to read, or for you to throw, should the opportunity arise.

School Library Photo Album

OUR LIBRARY
Lightbulbs changed last year; new doormat scheduled for this year.

LANDSCAPING
Aesthetics are so important in encouraging library use!

OUR FACILITIES
School libraries provide a combination of teaching space and resources.

our beautiful library

OUR STAFF
Generous salaries maintain high clothing standards, which promote our professionalism.

OUR STUDENTS
Lining up quietly before entering the library sets the tone for the lesson to follow.

AN ENERGIZED STAFF
An energized staff brainstorms at the end of another day working with children.

people make all the difference

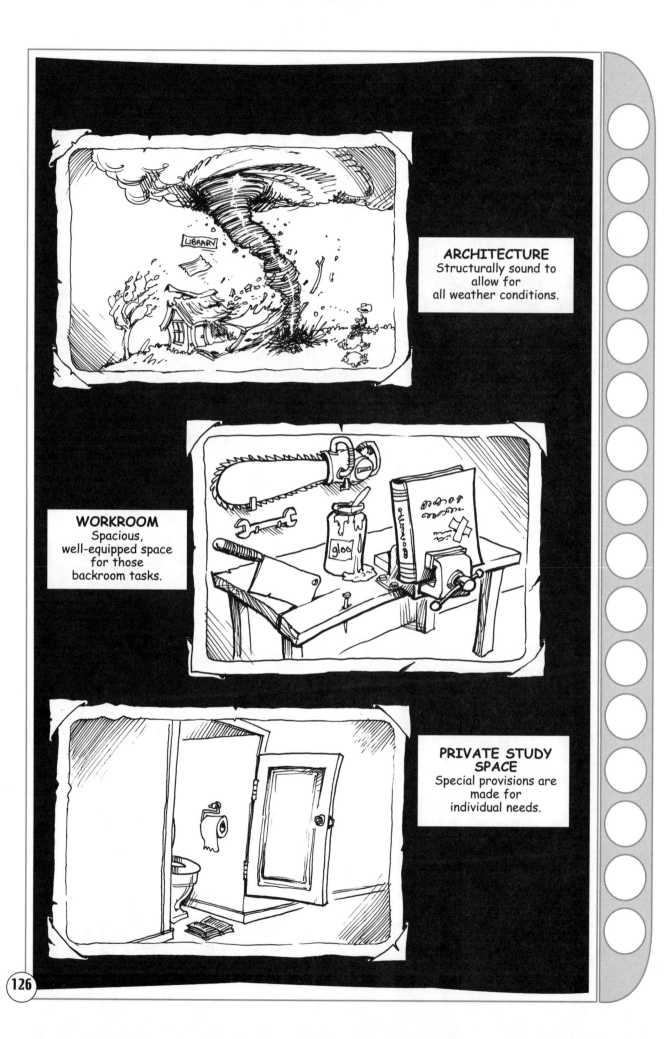

ARCHITECTURE
Structurally sound to
allow for
all weather conditions.

WORKROOM
Spacious,
well-equipped space
for those
backroom tasks.

**PRIVATE STUDY
SPACE**
Special provisions are
made for
individual needs.

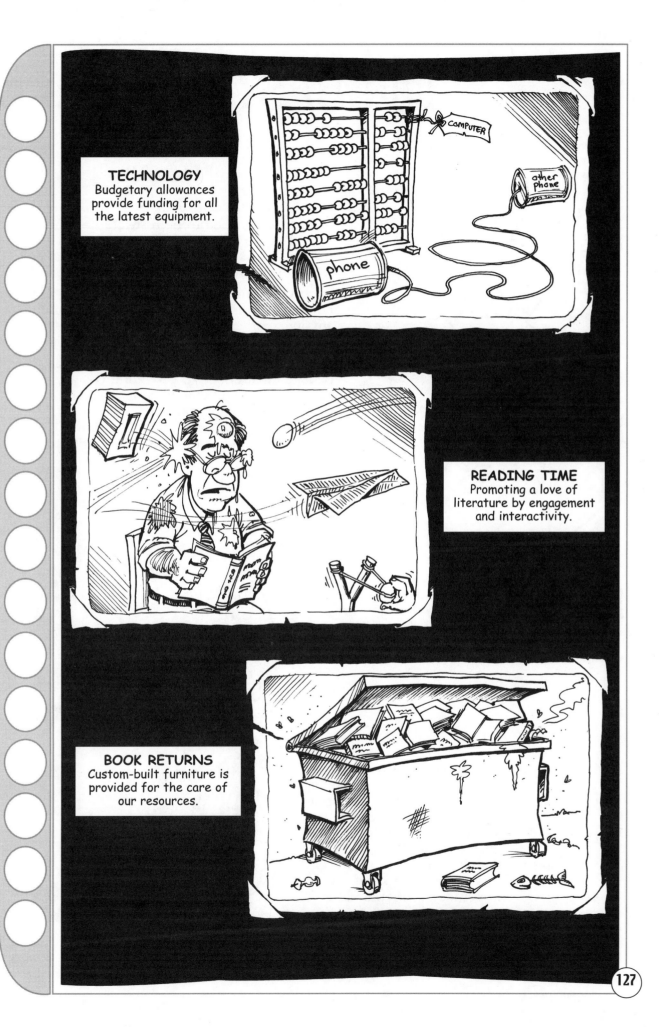

TECHNOLOGY
Budgetary allowances provide funding for all the latest equipment.

READING TIME
Promoting a love of literature by engagement and interactivity.

BOOK RETURNS
Custom-built furniture is provided for the care of our resources.

The *BEST* Aspects of

FREEDOM!

- The freedom to start work as early as you want to … no need to be restricted by the school's core starting time. Similarly, you are free to stay as long as you want after final bell when everyone has gone home.

- The freedom to select resources, as long as they conform to the selection policy, won't offend anyone, won't cause any controversy, and are cheap enough not to overstretch the budget.

- The freedom to organize your own day as you believe most effective, providing you are available for your scheduled lessons, the required meetings, your recess and lunch duties, and unforeseeable interruptions. The other five minutes are yours to do with as you wish.

PRIORITY PARKING!

- Because you get to work so early, you have your pick of the parking spaces—excluding the principal's spot; the deputy's; the clerical staff's; the head teacher's/coordinator's; the janitor's; disabled access spaces; spaces for people bigger than you and for teachers who have been at the school for more years than you; and spaces for visitors, parent volunteers, senior students, people with new cars, people with large cars ….

School Librarianship

SOCIAL LIFE!

- You'll never be lonely or bored. The phone will constantly ring, various people will come and visit you in the middle of your lunch break, and booksellers will eagerly seek you out.

- You will get to meet many interesting people who will want you to do various tasks for them. You will be able to find books for them, give advice on their research tasks, help their classes with Internet usage, refer them to other sources of information, etc. However, this will not be a reciprocal relationship.

LEGAL RIGHTS!

- You have the right to remain silent.
- You have the right to legal representation. Anything you say can and will be used against you.
- Your school board will support you ... yeah, right ....

THE EFFECTS OF BUDGET LIMITATIONS ON STUDENT RESEARCH

Try doing research using biased documents, stereotyped characteristics, and obsolete information.

My Research Project
by Billy Smith, age 11
July 7, 2003

<u>Aim:</u>
To investigate the role of women in recent scientific discovery.

<u>Method:</u>
Collect information from different library resources and present a report on the topic.

<u>Results:</u>
One day, MAN might walk on the moon (Scientific American, 1960). However, as the main occupation of women is either as teachers or nurses (Bureau of Statistics, 1937), very few women will be involved, except maybe as secretaries, until they get married.

Marie Curie was a famous woman scientist, but she died because of her work with science. If she had been home looking after her children (Sogynist, 1958), she would still be alive today.

The most important scientific discovery of the decade was most probably that of Liquid Paper, invented by Bette Graham in 1956 (Rand, 1958). Bette was a secretary who made a lot of typing mistakes, so she wasn't even a very good secretary.

Margaret Thatcher is the current prime minister of England (Thompson, 1986), but she used to be a scientist. She wasn't clever enough, so she left and became a politician. There are a lot of famous Russian women scientists listed on the Internet, but the information is in Russian, so I couldn't read it.

Grace Hopper was a famous computer scientist (Yale, 2001).

http/: Rear Admiral Dr. Grace Murray Hopper was a remarkable woman who grandly rose to the challenges of programming the first computers. During her lifetime as a leader in the field of software development concepts, she contributed to the transition from primitive programming techniques to the use of sophisticated compilers. She believed that "we've always done it that way" was not necessarily a good reason to continue to do so. Pursuing her belief that computer programs could be written in English, Admiral Hopper moved forward with the development for Univac of the B-O compiler, later known as FLOW-MATIC. It was designed to translate a language that could be used for typical business tasks like automatic billing and payroll calculation. Using FLOW-MATIC, Admiral Hopper and her staff were able to make the UNIVAC I and II "understand" twenty statements in English. When she recommended that an entire programming language be developed using English words, however, she "was told very quickly that [she] couldn't do this because computers didn't understand English." It was three years before her idea was finally accepted; she published her first compiler paper in 1952. Admiral Hopper actively participated in the first meetings to formulate specifications for a common business language. She was one of the two technical advisers to the resulting CODASYL Executive Committee, and several of her staff were members of the CODASYL Short Range Committee to define the basic COBOL language design. The design was greatly influenced by FLOW-MATIC. As one member of the Short Range Committee stated, "[FLOW-MATIC] was the only business-oriented programming language in use at the time COBOL development started ....Without FLOW-MATIC we probably never would have had a COBOL." The first COBOL specifications appeared in 1959. Admiral Hopper devoted much time to convincing business managers that English-language compilers such as FLOW-MATIC and COBOL were feasible. She participated in a public demonstration by Sperry Corporation and RCA of COBOL compilers and the machine independence they provided. After her brief retirement from the Navy, Admiral Hopper led an effort to standardize COBOL and to persuade the entire Navy to use this high-level computer language. With her technical skills, she lead her team to develop useful COBOL manuals and tools. With her speaking skills, she convinced managers that they should learn to use them. Another major effort in Admiral Hopper's life was the standardization of compilers. Under her direction, the Navy developed a set of programs and procedures for validating COBOL compilers. This concept of validation has had widespread impact on other programming languages and organizations; it eventually led to national and international standards and validation facilities for most programming languages. Recognition: Admiral Grace Murray Hopper received many awards and commendations for her accomplishments. In 1969, she was awarded the first ever Computer Science Man-of-the-Year Award from the Data Processing Management Association. In 1971, the Sperry Corporation initiated an annual award in her name to honor young computer professionals for their significant contributions to computer science. In 1973, she became the first person from the United States and the first woman of any nationality to be made a Distinguished Fellow of the British Computer Society.

Conclusion

Except for being the mother of scientists, and as secretaries of scientists, women don't really contribute much to scientific innovations. (Not counting Grace Hopper.)

References:

Bureau of Statistics (1937). Public Census Results.
Sogynist, M. I. (1957). The Role of Women in Science.
Rand Corporation (1958). Latest Technology in Office Practices. (Pamphlet Files).
Russian Women Scientists (2001). [online] http://www.day.kiev.ua/1997/29-97/society/r-osvi.htm.
Scientific American (1960). The Role of NASA.
Thompson, D. (1986). The Lives of British Politicians.
Yale University (2001). "Grace Hopper." [online] http://www.cs.yale.edu/homes/tap/Files/hopper-story.html.

OLYMPIC EVENTS FOR SCHOOL LIBRARIANS

FENCING

Evade questions regarding location of items that haven't been seen from before you started working in the library. Can be run in conjunction with Buck-Passing—it's so nice to have someone else to blame! The winner is judged on originality of answers, with the degree of difficulty considered.

20KM WALK

Walk from office to circulation desk, back to workroom, out to shelves, back to workroom, down to administration office, back to shelves, back to desk, and repeat 30 times. Complete one task at every checkpoint. Event must be finished in minimum time of six hours. The winner is the librarian who manages to complete the most amount of library administration work during the event.

BOXING

Pack culled books into boxes for donation to charities. Unpack to look for missing car keys that can't be found. Repack. The winner is the librarian who uses the least amount of packing tape.

SYNCHRONIZED CATALOGING

Teams of four librarians wearing plastic shower caps with flowers on their heads and book clamps over their noses catalog to classical music. This event is judged on fluidity of movement, degree of difficulty, and stupidity of headwear.

CLEAN AND JERK

Power-lift boxes of books to bench height for processing. The winner is the librarian with the least amount of back pain.

200M HURDLE

Run from library office to the administration office, jumping assorted bags, lunchboxes, and ill-placed garbage bins. On the way, jump over administrative barriers and through bureaucratic hoops. The winner is the librarian with the least number of bruises on his/her shins and the least amount of damage to his/her self-esteem.

ROWING

Put books on shelves in rows. Do it again after each class. Do it again after recess and lunchtime. Repeat each day. The winner is assessed according to the originality of utterances, with consideration of the ability to maintain some semblance of Dewey order.

WRESTLING

Make a list of things to do in a given day. Wrestle with the imperative to complete those tasks against assorted unforeseeable interruptions. The winner is the librarian who manages to get the greatest number of tasks completed while effectively dealing with everything else that was not on the original list.

MARATHON

Get into work early, boot-up computers, work on acquisitions, teach, consult with colleagues, miss all meal breaks, answer phone calls, and stay late to finish other tasks. This event is run over five consecutive days, then a two-day break, and repeated for a minimum of forty weeks. The winner is everyone who manages to make it to retirement age.

CHALKPUT

Hurl small pieces of chalk at large groups of children who are not listening to instructions in programmed lessons. The winner is judged on throwing style, degree of difficulty, and accuracy.

Note: Males and females compete on equal terms.
Venue: Any typical school library.

Interactive Books

Kids in libraries head for the computers before the shelves of books because computers are fun for kids. No one disputes the many benefits of books over the benefits of the Internet, but let's face it: Books are frankly quite boring animals. They need spicing up so that each tome is an adventure beyond text. The pop-up concept of early childhood books is only the beginning of interesting books for the new millennium ....

The Jack-in-the-Book: One "secret" page, when turned, releases a spring mechanism that projects a character from the book (e.g., E.T.).

Rabbit Out-of-the-Book: Part of the book has been hollowed out and conceals a collapsible toy rabbit that can be pulled out at will. This may be a little tame for older readers, so a more ferocious animal can be substituted.

Illuminated Issue: Combining the concepts of LCD screens and ancient manuscripts, illustrated pages can be backlit with battery operated "magic slate" technology, although this could make the books a little thick.

The Volvelle: By using rotating circular cards, astronomy books have long used this technique for demonstrating constellation movements and other stellar phenomena. Adapting this principle, books can add spiked metal edges to provide the added excitement of a buzz saw.

Micro Monographs: A challenge for any publisher, these books extend the concept of the mini-book. The books require a microscope and that the pages be turned with a needle; kids will get many hours of reading pleasure (not to mention blinding headaches that will keep them quiet for many hours afterward).

Interactive Books

Hologram Handbooks: At the high end of the budget spectrum, this book uses a built-in hologram projector to show illustrations at each relevant page. Two in use at the same time can become interactive with each other, and a whole library full creates a virtual reality that beats the heck out of the standard computer play parlors.

Boomerang Book: This self-returning item is a surefire winner with libraries because it will mail itself back when it becomes due. If purchased for private use, it can be set to put itself back on a shelf, thus reducing housework, particularly in teenagers' rooms.

The Reeking Reader: Specifically designed for libraries, this book emits an increasingly foul odor as the due date approaches to remind patrons that they have to get that book back soon. If the due date is exceeded, the stench will be so overpowering that the neighbors will become aware that there is an overdue book next door and will complain to the authorities.

The Bathroom Book: A handy book for multitasking. As you're sitting down anyway, indulge your reading whims. No need for a book mark—just dispose of the part you've consumed, and on your next visit just pick up where you left off. Not suitable for shared facilities.

The Really Big Book: Here's reading material in which you can really lose yourself. Its dimensions make it impossible to misplace, too.

The Backpack Book: Ideal for travelers, this book comes with detachable strapping, so it won't take up valuable luggage space. This also makes it very accessible for unexpected delays at airports, railway stations, or rest rooms.

Overdue Notices from Famous School Librarians

Sweet Valley High School Library

Dear Mr./Mrs./Ms./Dr./Other

_____:

Your son/daughter/ward has the following books overdue:

1.
2.
3.

Therefore, we have confiscated her lipstick/his comb until such time as the books are returned or paid for. As this will severely limit their social life, I'm sure you will ensure that swift action is taken. The results of delaying the return or payment may cause catastrophic long-term psychological damage.

Yours Sincerely,

HOGWARTS LIBRARY

Dear Parent/Guardian/Witch/Warlock/Other:

Your son/daughter/ward/familiar has the following resources overdue:

1.
2.
3.

Until these resources are returned, _____ has been banned from watching and/or playing in all Quiddich Games, having been (literally) grounded.

Yours Sincerely,

Bedrock BC 3002

Dear Family Facilitator:

Your v.2 has the following materials overdue:
1.
2.
3.
If these materials are not returned forthwith, and in the original condition in which they were lent, notwithstanding damage caused by fair and reasonable use, together with the original packaging, we will alter all your credit card passwords, cut utilities to your domicile, withdraw all technical support from your place of employment, and send you a reminder in 10 days.

The terms and conditions of this demand are not negotiable.

If you are not the intended recipient of this notice, please return to sender.

Yours Sincerely,

 Microsoft Academy Library

South Park Elementary

Hey There, Parents and/or Guardians,

We were very surprised to find out that _____ has actually borrowed a book. We didn't know he/she could read, let alone find the library.

The book was supposed to be brought back weeks ago, but what the heck! Since no one else ever borrowed anything from here before, we want _____ to keep it.

Do you think he/she could get some of his/her friends to borrow a book, too?

Lewis

'SHE'S IN CHARGE OF THE OVERDUES!'

INTRODUCTORY LIBRARY LESSONS

Yeah, some understanding of Dewey is important. And, OK, so is OPAC operation. But aren't we jumping the gun a little here? What basics should librarians teach before attempting bibliographic instruction, let alone the principles of information literacy?

LESSON 1: DOORS

TEACHER NOTES	Doors are for entering and leaving the building. They are not conversation pits or bag storage areas. Although the lintel makes a good swing-bar, it is not designed for this purpose. Some doors open and close automatically—this is to allow you to enter and leave, not for the amusement of the indolent.
CLASSWORK	• Identify a door • Demonstrate the use of a door • Locate doors on a map of the library • Draw a door • Make a model of a door

LESSON 2: CHAIRS

TEACHER NOTES	Chairs are a type of furniture designed for sitting purposes. It is unwise to stand on them because they sometimes fall sideways or backward. Most chairs in libraries have four *legs*, which should be kept in contact with the floor. You should not throw chairs, as they lack the aerodynamics of aircraft. They also have more projecting parts than a ball and are therefore slightly dangerous when airborne. Although chairs make a convenient depository for used chewing gum, this will present a hazard to your health, particularly if you are caught.
CLASSWORK	• Identify a chair in a group of other furniture • Demonstrate the use of a chair • Describe different types of chairs • Label a diagram of a chair

LESSON 3: TABLES

TEACHER NOTES	Tables are designed to hold reading and writing tools, such as books, pens, and paper. When you sit at a table, feet should be placed on the floor, unless you are going to use them for writing purposes. Tables do make good platforms for performances. Unfortunately, the library cannot supply sufficient improvised stages for everyone. Therefore, in the interests of fairness to all, libraries do not permit you to stand on tables except in times of flood.
CLASSWORK	• Locate a table in the library • Demonstrate placement of feet under the table • Synthesize the combined use of a chair (from previous lesson) with the use of a table • Describe consequences of improper table use (may be written or by oral presentation)

INTRODUCTORY LIBRARY LESSONS

LESSON 4: SHELVES

TEACHER NOTES	Library shelves are designed for book storage. Gaps between groups of books are quite normal in a library. There is no need for you to fill these gaps with books from other shelves or with food scraps. Rows of shelves are arranged in libraries in a particular order. Librarians like it this way. Changing this arrangement can make librarians very sad, if not downright angry. The rows of shelves are placed in groups called *bays*. In a library, the word *bay* doesn't refer to the making of animal noises. Bays are placed in groups called *runs*. The word *run* doesn't refer to library user movement through the library. Fast movement should be restricted to eyes because this is less distracting for other library users and causes less damage to both people and equipment.
CLASSWORK	• Indicate location of a shelf • Take ONE book off of a shelf • Replace book on shelf in SAME position • Drill and practice: WALKING past shelf

LESSON 5: BOOKS

TEACHER NOTES	Books are made of paper, which may not be very robust. The pages of a book are glued, stapled, or sown together, and they may not be very robust. On the outside of library books are a number of stickers (barcodes and spine labels), which may not be very robust. The books are purchased, processed, and administered by the librarians, who may not be very robust.
CLASSWORK	• Locate a dictionary • Look up the word *robust* • Construct a draft letter to the library staff, apologizing for all previous, current, and future damage to library books.

NEXT SET OF LESSONS

LESSON 6: Newspapers, Journals, and Magazines
LESSON 7: Videos as Information Sources
LESSON 8: Photocopiers, Scanners, and Buttocks
LESSON 9: Librarians Are People, Too
LESSON 10: What Your Parents Didn't Tell You About Librarians

NEW PORTAL FULFILLS STUDENT RESEARCH NEEDS
www.emailandchat.com

TECHNOLOGIA:

APRIL 6, 2020

The Government Education Corporation, in a bid to boost stock prices for its Schools Portfolio, has released the ultimate portal for students' research needs.

www.emailandchat.com will reside on the government's education server and will provide students with every possible link students could want or need.

Having completed rigorous beta-testing, the website has received rave reviews from the survey group of senior students. "Rooly Kool" was the most frequently emailed comment received from no less than 88 of the 90 students used in the test sample. The remaining two comments were "IMHOROFL" and "fentistec." These comments are still being analyzed.

Parent groups were also surveyed. They confirmed that the students seemed to be heavily engrossed in the website on nights before research assignments were due, and therefore must be getting good information from the portal.

It appears that only teachers remain unimpressed. An official spokesperson from the Teacher Protection Group stated that there was no discernible change in the quality of research being submitted for assessment.

Justin Thyme, media spokesperson for the corporation, stated that many millions of research dollars had been spent in ensuring that the students were equipped with the best possible resource to suit their needs.

At the media launch of the portal, Thyme produced collations of cached sited that had been gathered from Internet-enabled computers in school libraries.

"Clearly, this is the material most used by students to support their studies," Thyme stated. Future additions to the website will include music downloads and links for online dating, as these were also shown to be highly used areas of the Internet.

Librarian Spreads Suffering and Misery

MARCH 8, 2008

TINYTOWN

In an unprecedented attack on innocent youth, the school librarian at Tinytown High School has mailed out overdue notices to students of the school with outstanding library loans.

Asked why she felt it necessary to terrorize the community with thinly veiled threats of library fines, the school librarian [name withheld pending legal action] stated that it was "not an unusual procedure; many schools do this on a regular basis."

However, when pressed for the names of other school librarians who repeated this despicable act, the school librarian declined to provide any further information.

Local police interviewed the principal of the school, following complaints by parents of harassment. Mr. Courtney Fische, a spokesman for the school, stated that the principal was too upset for an interview, but he read from a prepared statement.

Quoting from the official handbook, Fische stated the "in cases of longstanding overdue books, the librarian may use professional judgment in contacting the parents and guardians of the students."

A parent of one of the victims, who asked to "remain ambiguous," sobbed as she told the story of how she opened the mail that morning, only to discover that things had gone terribly wrong at the school.

"The book is only 26 months overdue, and I think that the fact that it's only one volume of a 30-volume encyclopedia set should be taken into account. After all, they've still got the other 29 volumes. How would you like to have to cough up $6.50 for one lousy library book?"

It is believed that up to six overdue notices may have been mailed. Investigations are continuing.

SCHOOL STUDENTS FEAR READING

**Somewhere Valley,
JULY 12, 2006**

Students at Somewhere Valley Comprehensive School were forced to hide behind comics and video games, when the school's librarian wheeled a trolley of books up to the door and knocked.

The vehicle was heavily laden with a class set of dictionaries, a selection of quality literature, and a large unidentified box believed to possibly contain brochures on conducting online research.

As the student council members closed in and removed the books, the librarian tried to justify her behavior by stating that "wide reading promotes literacy, which in turn assists in the learning process—learning being a language-based process."

The students then broke into uncontrollable laughter, some of them having to be sent home in a debilitated condition. Band-Aids were issued to a number of students who fell over from excessive mirth.

Claude Backe, a spokesman for the education authority, stated that steps were being taken to ensure that books would remain in libraries where they belong, and added that all book trolleys would be removed from school libraries immediately.

"If this sort of thing is allowed to happen, we will have children reading all over the place, and the resultant outbreak of literacy would severely affect the economy. What would happen to the entertainment industry?" Backe emphasized.

It is believed that reading instructions on how to make a "school bookmobile" on a library website may have provoked this incident. Steps are now being taken to remove the website and to prosecute the authors.

The school librarian signed an agreement that she would not leave the library again and would never force students to read against their will.

Student Victim of Sadistic Librarian

Metropolis:
November 3, 2011

Sixteen-year-old Damien Galah, a student of Metropolis Middle School, sat ashen-faced before members of the mass media. His story was one of terror; his classmates rallied around him for support.

The day started for Damien much as any other. He arrived late for school, kicking over a full garbage can on the way to class. He engaged in the usual playground roughhousing at recess, and he made the mandatory visit to the school principal at the start of lunchtime to have his conduct card signed.

Approaching the librarian, Damien gave him a copy of his assignment and asked "for the books." There was no way Damien could have known that the librarian would then ask him where he had already looked because the young lad hadn't used the library before, having only been a student at the school for the last four years.

Being taken to the OPACs and shown how to do a search was not on Damien's agenda, but clearly the librarian had ulterior motives.

An explanation of the research cycle followed. This inhumane treatment continued, with online databases then being flashed before him.

For a young man who had only wanted the books handed to him, Damien was close to the breaking point.

When questioned by the media, Damien stated that he believed that the librarian had a history of this type of abuse. Unfortunately, there were no coherent witnesses to support the allegation, although there were many offers of statements. Frequent comments such as "school sucks" and "I never liked him much anyway" were heard.

Sarah Bellum, the school counselor, was inundated with other students in an outbreak of mass hysteria. Other counselors were brought to the school, and a counseling hotline was set up. Ms. Bellum said that she had previously counseled students after they had been asked for their borrowing cards by the library staff.

Strikeback!
The Rubric for Appraising the Appraisers

OUTCOME 1: Provides sufficient financial support for efficient, effective information services.

INDICATORS	ACHIEVEMENT LEVEL
• There is no budget to support the library. • Budget is sufficient for library staff to subscribe to a newsletter. • Budget sufficient for the purchase of 10–50 secondhand books per year. • Budget sufficient for the purchase of 10–50 new books per year. • Budget is sufficient for library staff to misappropriate enough funds for a sandwich from the cafeteria. • Budget allows for a formal acquisitions program, support of all subjects throughout the client area, a quality literature collection to suit all levels of ability and interests, and maintenance of all equipment and resources.	1. The finance committee knows that the library exists. 2. The finance committee members have actually been to the library. 3. At least one member of the finance committee has borrowed a library book in the last 10 years. 4. The finance committee has allowed sufficient budgetary allowances to enable the library to function.

OUTCOME 2: Clerical support is provided to assist in circulation, processing, and other duties to enable the librarian to complete professional-level activities, such as bibliographic instruction.

INDICATORS	ACHIEVEMENT LEVEL
• There is no clerical support. • The local vandals assist with culling, using the trial-by-fire method. • A volunteer parent turns up occasionally. • Several volunteer parents turn up occasionally. • A large number of volunteer parents turn up regularly, and they sit around and talk. • A member of clerical staff actually is allocated to the library. • A member of clerical staff is trained in library procedures and is allocated to the library permanently.	1. The administrators know that the library exists. 2. The administrators know that clerical support is required. 3. The administrators provide insufficient clerical support. 4. The administrators provide sufficient clerical support. 5. The administrators provide excessive clerical support.

Strikeback!
The Rubric for Appraising the Appraisers

OUTCOME 3: The value and importance of information literacy is recognized and is integrated throughout the library's instructional programs.

INDICATORS	ACHIEVEMENT LEVEL
• No one has set an authentic research task in the last five years. • At least one teacher has set an authentic research assignment in the last five years. • Multiple teachers have set research assignments in the last five years. • Classroom teachers occasionally consult with the teacher librarian. • Classroom teachers regularly consult with the teacher librarian. • Classroom teachers always consult with the teacher librarian. • The teacher librarian has timetabled "Library Lessons," the outcomes of which aren't included in the school's reporting procedures. • The teacher librarian has a flexible schedule and works with students and teachers on a as-needed basis.	1. No one outside the library has heard of information literacy. 2. Teaching staff has heard of information literacy, but they believe that it will create more work for them. 3. Teaching staff has embraced the concepts of information literacy and has set authentic research tasks. They understand the importance of such issues as plagiarism and attend in-services on information literacy on their own time/at their own cost.

OUTCOME 4: Provides funding and qualified personnel to maintain computer hardware and software to enable effective access to digital resources.

INDICATORS	ACHIEVEMENT LEVEL
• The library has a computer. • The library has electricity to run the computer. • The computer actually works. • The library has several computers that actually work. • The library computers have an Internet connection. • The library computers can actually access the Internet. • There is a technology maintenance schedule to ensure that all computers stay working.	1. The administrators know that a lot of libraries now have computers. 2. The administrators know that some information is digitally delivered. 3. The administrators understand the importance of ICT. 4. The administrators ensure that the library is appropriately equipped with regard to digital sources.

Strikeback!
The Rubric for Appraising the Appraisers

OUTCOME 5: Provides structures and funding to promote an appreciation of literature.

INDICATORS	ACHIEVEMENT LEVEL
• The library has some literature to appreciate. • The library has a broad range of quality literature. • School schedules allow for access to the literature. • Reading time is provided. • Reading time is provided outside the scheduled "roll call/homeroom" time.	1. School administrators have read a book "for pleasure" in the past 10 years. 2. School administrators have read at least one book a year for the past 10 years. 3. School administrators know the difference between *Readers' Digest* magazine and a Booker Prize-winner.

OUTCOME 6: Where an appraisal is undertaken of the teacher librarian/library media specialist/school librarian and the school library services, an appropriate assessor is engaged.

INDICATORS	ACHIEVEMENT LEVEL
• The assessor has a postgraduate degree in librarianship. • The assessor has multiple degrees in librarianship. • The assessor has specialist qualifications in teacher librarianship. • The assessor has worked in a school library in the past three years. • The assessor regularly updates qualifications in school library sciences. • The assessor regularly attends in-servicing in school librarianship to keep abreast of the latest developments. • The assessor has demonstrated both aptitude and ability in accessing teacher librarians and school library services. • The assessor can produce evidence of understanding of the issues involved in contemporary school librarianship.	1. The assessor is not qualified to assess school library staff or school library services. 2. The assessor is qualified to assess school library staff and school library services (requires ALL of the indicators shown). 

Biblia Looks At Library Memoranda

Technology

From: The Director, Technology Division
To: All Technology Section Heads

To ensure power saving over the school holiday period, please instruct all personnel concerned to shut down and turn off all workstations before leaving on the final workday before the holidays commence.

❦ DISTRICT OFFICE ❧

From: District Office
To: School Principals

You are hereby warned that computers in your school are to be shut down. This is the final notice due to the upcoming holidays. Ensure your staff are informed of this concerting issue.

From: Technology Unit 1
To: All District Offices

Workstations must be turned off before holiday shut down. This warning is for the final day, as instructed by the director, who is concerned about this issue.

From: The Principal
To: All Head Teachers

I have received notification that computers are not to be used in the school. Until this issue is clarified after the concert, instruct all staff to disconnect the computers immediately and make appropriate arrangements for alternative methods.

From: Head Teacher
To: Teacher Librarian

Computers will no longer be used in the library. Pack them for indefinite storage and retrieve old card catalogs. A concert will be held, presumably to raise funds for new filing cabinets.

Biblia Looks At Library Memoranda
Budget Cuts

From: Financial Services Department

To: School Library Staff

Recent media announcements pertaining to the increase in budget allocations to schools have created the impression that school libraries may benefit from increased allocations. However, the extra funding is not directed at school libraries. In fact, the following cost-cutting in this area will come into effect immediately:

Tattle tapes and tags, together with electronic detection machinery, will no longer be purchased. Exit control will be enactioned by the use of large dogs, who will reside next to exits. As most school libraries only have one doorway, the dogs will also act as food inhibitors; this will additionally provide nourishment for the dogs by removing contraband (food) items from children as they enter the library.

2. Electricity bills for lighting in libraries will be reduced by turning off all lights during daylight hours. Where library users express difficulty in reading due to this procedure, library staff will direct patrons to the lighting stand, where torches and batteries are available at recommended retail prices. Students and staff are also permitted to bring their own lighting equipment, although campfires in the library are to be discouraged.

Where bats take up residence in these libraries, they are to be cataloged as realia and included in stocktake. Due to the difficulty in attaching barcodes to glow worms, these may be excluded from stocktake. Any mushrooms found growing in these conditions may be harvested and sold at the library snack bar.

3. Air-conditioning systems, where in place, should not be turned on during the summer. Library users may purchase personal, battery-operated fans at the library gift shop. Similarly, the use of heaters is now prohibited—the gift shop should stock a selection of blankets, jackets, and sweaters for purchase.

4. Recent audits have shown that books are a major expense in library budgeting. This should cease immediately. Alternate sources should be sought where books can be obtained for free. Nursing homes and hospitals generally have books in their waiting rooms. Similarly, journals and periodicals may be obtained free of charge from dentists' and doctors' waiting rooms. Where empty spaces appear on library shelving, promotional material for books can be cut out of newspapers and folded to look like a book. In the event that contracts for standing orders exist, the books purchased at discounted rates may be sold at recommended retail price in the library gift shop.

5. The library staff should fix minor maintenance work, such as faulty power points or collapsed roofing. Recognizing the fact that few library workers are trained in this area, financial service's website will shortly feature a "How to ... " section to provide online support. Should a problem arise that is not covered by this website, you should fill out the online form and wait for a reply. Expected turnaround time for this service will be approximately 30 working days.

Although these cutbacks and changes may seem drastic at the moment, the benefits will soon become obvious. Schools will be able to allocate more funds to visible, external improvements [e.g., gardens, new fencing, etc.], plus the publication of glossy brochures promoting the school's facilities, which will greatly improve the profile of the school within the community.

Biblia Looks At Library Memoranda
Communications

From: Human Relations Division
To: Teacher Librarians

It has been brought to our attention that frustration levels are rising in school libraries due to an inability to accurately express emotions in a politically correct manner. Therefore, the following examples have been provided to address this issue.
When asked to complete yet another task not in your job description, the correct response is:
I'll just cancel my weekend plans. No worries.

"Get bent" is no way to win friends and influence people and further creates the impression you have a life outside the workplace. When asked to do the impossible, the correct response is:
I'm not sure that is feasible, not "Get Real!"

You have accepted a position where undertaking the impossible, and achieving it, is part of your job description.
When told that you will be losing even more clerical support hours, the correct response is:
I enjoy a challenge! not "You've got to be kidding."
We must all realize that cost–cutting is a vital survival mechanism in schools, and just because the clerical time is taken from the library before anywhere else is no reason to become hostile.

When a deadline is moved up from next week to tomorrow, the correct response is:
I'll reschedule my other tasks, not "Why didn't you tell me sooner?"
This will assist others in confirming that their idea of what is important is more valid than yours and will ensure that you will be prepared to drop everything to accommodate the poor organization of others.

When a school–wide issue arises and an after–hours meeting is called, the correct response is: *Yes, this needs to be discussed*, not "Not another damn meeting!"
This is valuable networking time for teacher librarians, and the perceived necessity to collect your children from their school, or to prepare the evening meal for your family, should be secondary to anything related to the promotion of teacher librarianship.

If a colleague approaches you in the middle of a major library task to chat about something completely inane, the correct response is:
How fascinating!, not "Tell someone who cares."
You can never tell when that person might be in a position to promote the positive aspects of the school library. After all, you can always stay late (again) to finish the interrupted task, happy in the knowledge that your colleague has left 30 minutes before the final bell.

When approached by a senior executive of the school who wishes to discuss how overloaded he/she is with tedious administrative tasks, the correct response is:
Would you like me to take care of that for you? not "So What?"
Remember that this person controls your library budget and would not have taken time out of his/her busy schedule to talk with you unless he/she wanted something.
We hope that you have found these suggestions helpful, and look forward to hearing how you have implemented them into your everyday work practices.

Dear Biblia ... The Advice Column

Dear Biblia:

Dear Biblia,
What is the correct protocol for providing library services? Should I attend to staff before students, or serve in order of request?

Ms. Manners

Dear Ms. Manners,

It very much depends on the identity of the patrons. If it is a teacher who has been supportive in the past, and a student who has proved troublesome, the answer is obvious.

However, if the descriptions are reversed, feign a nausea attack and run to the rest room. They will go away if you stay in there for long enough.

⋆⟶◎⟵⋆

Dear Biblia,

I open the school library for an hour before school and an hour after school; I am open every recess and lunchtime, as well as right through the day. And yet when I want to close for two weeks for stocktake, everyone complains. Is there some way I can address this issue?

Tired and Confused

Dear Tired and Confused,

You have only yourself to blame. You've provided an excellent service, which your school cannot do without, and it's quite rightly recognized that the loss of two weeks' access is a serious concern.

I would recommend that you adjust your operations to prepare your school for this loss.

During the first term, shut the library completely for one day each week. During the second term, close for one week each month. By the third term, they'll be surprised that the library is open at all—so allocate one hour each day when access will be provided (e.g., 3:00 A.M. to 4:00 A.M.). By the fourth term, you can do as you please, including stocktake.

⋆⟶◎⟵⋆

Dear Biblia,

I can't seem to get the teachers at this school to return their overdue books. The kids are fine, but what should I do about the staff?

Concerned

Dear Concerned,

You must give them plenty of warning, in most instances at least 20 overdue notices. A friendly reminder is always appropriate, and some school librarians find that attaching a chocolate to the notice may help. This will not bring immediate results because teachers are very busy people and often don't have time to read little notes. You must be patient, but you'll find that by letting the air out of their car tires, then sticking the 21st notice under their windshield wipers, they will find that couple of minutes to read your communication and respond. *[Hint: Don't park YOUR car at school.]*

⋆⟶◎⟵⋆

Dear Biblia,

I've been trying to get an appointment with my supervisor for weeks to discuss some issues within our school library. He's always busy or out of his office. How can I get him to give me an appointment?

Pushed Aside

This is an automated reply. The recipient is unavailable at this time, but will get back to you soon.

Peter Hughes' Brochure for Teachers

The following pointers are offered to those seeking to excel in abusing the facilities of the library ....

1. Reserve the library by calling up a minute prior to the lesson ... better still, just turn up without any notice at all. There's nothing like spontaneity!

2. *Don't restrict the students' individuality by asking them to line up outside the library ... just pour in like a horde of Assyrians on the rampage!*

3. Don't bother preparing the students for the assignment by discussing expectations, guidelines, etc. Wait until you get into the library to bark a few ill-considered instructions at them over the noise all the other library users are making to get themselves heard.

4. *Be deliberately vague about what the aim of the assignment is. For example, just tell them to "find something out" about the chosen topic. Don't be specific about what you want them to research. Guidelines are so limiting!*

5. Don't keep your class in one area of the library ... let them mingle and socialize with/disturb one of your colleagues' classes. Share your lack of organization!

6. *Don't discuss the assignment beforehand with the librarian ... but demand he drop everything when you arrive and ask him to give an impromptu explanation of the Dewey decimal system and the meaning of life.*

7. Don't expect your students to use the full splendor of the library's resources ... why bother with the catalog, periodicals, A/V resources, CD-ROMs, online databases, or the Internet—when you can fall back on the 1948 edition of *World Book*. (Actually, that was a joke ... I took the 1948 edition off the shelves last week!)

8. *Library lessons are excellent opportunities for catching up on local news. Relax with a cup of coffee and the local newspaper ... if you can get to it before your students do ... after all, it's bound to have a potted biography of Tycho Brahe amid its squalid pages!*

9. Don't inhibit your students' creativity by expecting them to focus on the task in hand ... foster the jellyfish approach to learning ... drifting here and there in the hope that some morsel of information will present itself to their voracious thirst for knowledge!

10. *Don't actively supervise your students and don't be aware of what they're up to ... it's so much more fun to find out about scratched CDs and torn pages after the event!*

11. Finally, wait until after the bell has rung to get the students to pack up, borrow items, tidy their desks, etc. Enjoy the harassed look on the librarian's face as he tries to loan books, to ensure items are placed on the return trolley, and to answer the phone at the same time ... no doubt some other malignant soul is on the line with another group of ... er, "students!"

At the time of writing, Peter Hughes was the teacher librarian at Parkes High School, Australia.

What Librarians Can Learn From Kids

- Regardless of the original color, flavor, or brand, used chewing gum has no aesthetic appeal.

- There are 234,496,493 possible places for any given book, even in a small library.

- The more expensive the set of encyclopedias, the higher the chance of a single volume getting ripped off.

- Tear-proof book covering has not been invented yet.

- Barcode wands or guns produce strange reflections in people's eyes.

- All types and grades of paper absorb finger grease equally.

- Barcodes can be easily removed with a scalpel blade, scissors, or chain saw.

- Published borrowing limits are only a starting point for negotiation.

- Reference interviews violate international conventions on privacy.

- There is no such thing as a "gentle" book return chute.

- "No food or drink" signs mean different things to patrons and librarians.

- The word "quiet" has no meaning for anyone under the age of 18.

- Security systems aren't.

- Direction signs don't.

- "Graffiti Proof" isn't.

"HEY... YOU FOUND MY BOOKMARK!"

RULES FOR SCHOOL LIRARIES

✔ No library user will damage, deface, bend, fold, or mutilate any resource in this library, without the consent of the library staff.

✔ Computer use is restricted to those times when the computers are not under repair. You should note that this means you can use them from 2:00 P.M. to 4:00 P.M. on Wednesdays and 9:00 A.M. to 11:00 A.M. on Fridays. The Internet is available when the server is functioning. Generally, the network does not operate on Wednesdays or Fridays due to routine maintenance.

✔ A number of board games are available for use in the library. We have three chessboards (but no pieces) and a Monopoly set without a board. There is also a set of 37 playing cards and 5 dice. Students are encouraged to borrow the whole box of game pieces and create their own game.

✔ Lending of any equipment or resources is restricted to those who have proven that they are trustworthy and reliable. There are currently three students who may borrow. If you wish to have your previous misdemeanors and transgressions forgiven and to be considered for this privilege, collect an application form from the library staff. Please fill out the application form in triplicate, attach a copy of your birth certificate, together with a testimonial from another library, and present the documentation to the library staff. The progress of your application will be mailed to you next year.

'OKAY...OKAY!'

Prayer for School Librarians

Lord, grant me the Serenity
To accept that the book is lost forever;
The Courage to refuse
A loan when there's an existing overdue;
The Patience required
Not to throttle my classroom colleagues
(Even when they really deserve it);
The Strength to keep battling on
In the face of all the barriers that ignorance
builds;
And the Wisdom to know
That although my good work is unlikely to
be
Adequately recognized,
It is still worth doing.

APPENDIX I

GLOSSARY

TERM	ENCYCLOPEDIA DEFINITION	REAL MEANING
Acquisitions	Library department responsible for the actual ordering and purchasing of materials being added to the library's collection.	Mail center for promotional flyers and catalogs or coffee stop for booksellers, where potentially valuable additions to the collection are rejected on the grounds of cost.
Barcode Label	A small label comprised of vertical lines that contain machine-readable data; each item acquired by the library receives a bar code label with a unique number.	Souvenir of daring, much prized by library users.
Blurb	A brief summary or description of a work printed on the book jacket, publisher's catalog, or advertisement to entice potential purchasers.	The stuff you have to read the day before an exam on the book.
Book	1. A written or printed work of fiction or nonfiction, usually on sheets of paper fastened or bound together within covers. 2. A number of sheets of blank or ruled paper bound together for writing, recording business transactions, etc. 3. A division of a literary work, especially one of the larger divisions.	1. Paper-based material inaccessible due to indeterminable location. 2. Electronic version of paper-based material, inaccessible due to computer failure.
Borrow	To take or obtain with the promise to return the same or an equivalent.	To take or return with the intention of eventually returning same or equivalent, if and when convenient.
Carrel	A table for one reader, providing a somewhat secluded study area by means	of front and side screening. A nice hiding place or an unsupervised area for mischief.
Circulation	The library department responsible for activities connected with the lending and return of library materials, including reshelving, searching, rush requesting for material in process, etc.	Place where photocopying change is provided and directions to the toilets are given. Often "Abuse Central."
Hard Copy	Data printed on paper, in human-readable form, usually by a computer. Compare with soft copy, which is an image on a computer screen.	Large volume of text written out by hand when the photocopier is broken.
Hold	A request that an item be kept for a patron until he/she can pick it up.	Storage for patrons who are poorly organized.

APPENDIX I

GLOSSARY

TERM	ENCYCLOPEDIA DEFINITION	REAL MEANING
Internet	Vast interconnection of computers for information and communication access.	Really cool place to download games and mobile phone ring-tones and to email friends; provides access to graphics the library won't buy.
Journal	A periodical publication in which researchers report the results of their work to their peer community. Articles are reviewed by an editorial board of scholars in the field prior to acceptance for publication (*see also* refereed journal) and generally include an abstract and numerous citations to previous work.	The type of magazine you don't read unless you have to write a paper.
Librarian	1. A person trained in library science and engaged in library service. 2. A person in charge of a library, especially the chief administrative officer of a library. 3. A person who is in charge of any specialized body of literature, as a collection of musical scores.	1. A person qualified for a managerial role in a library who does all the stuff that no one else with the same qualifications will do.
Library	A collection of books or other written or printed materials or digitally stored data, as well as the facility in which they are housed and the institution that is responsible for their maintenance.	A collection of resources and equipment that librarians would like to be borrowed, then returned, but in the same condition in which they were lent.
Library School	Educational institution providing professional training for librarians (*see also* library).	Place where theory is supported by practical experience, none of which prepares you for the real world.
Open Access	Book stacks to which users have free access to browse and retrieve items on their own, as opposed to closed stacks.	Self-service aisles, but without the shopping carts.
"See" Reference	A note in a catalog used to guide the user from a heading that is not used in the catalog to one that is used.	Tells patron to ask at the desk.
Telnet	A program that allows users to login to other computers on the Internet via TCP/IP.	Method of using the Internet, but lacking any graphics, sound files, or cool effects. Might as well read a book ....

APPENDIX II

QUICK GUIDE TO PROFESSIONAL ASSOCIATIONS

ALN (Anodora Library Network): No members at the moment.

AUL (Association of Unemployable Librarians): For those lacking references or professional referees due to their recurring insistence on sharing their opinions of their supervisors with the same.

CATCLAW (Catalogers Calling Loudly After Work): Social group for catalogers who want to be really outrageous.

CGLHH (Collegial Group for Librarians in High Heels): Gender-indifferent group welcoming those who suffer from sore feet but who refuse to conform to stereotypical footwear.

LiFoC (Librarians in Favor of Censorship): The two existing members seek expressions of interest from any like-minded individuals, or indeed any evidence of their existence.

LCN (Library Chat Net): Online community with the sole purpose of regular debriefing. There are no protocols to follow, nor are there language limitations. Just let it all hang out ….

MLG (Mali Literacy Group): Promotes reading as an educational experience.

MELFWP (Middle Eastern Librarians for World Peace): The world's oldest library association; in continuous existence for more than 2000 years. Currently updating original charter.

NVLVC (Non-Voluntary Library Volunteers Collective): Lawbreakers who have been sentenced to community service hours in libraries are invited to register complaints on the grounds of "cruel and unusual punishment" (e.g., work loads; working conditions; difficulties with patrons, administrators, and librarians). These details can be used to commute your sentence to the softer option of hard labor in a government correctional facility.

TLSG (Technophobic Librarians Support Group): For those librarians missing the old card catalogs and who are used to tearing open paper envelopes to read their mail. Twenty-four-hour crisis line, regular counseling sessions, and brick wall for head-banging are included in membership fees.

ULIB (Union of Librarians with Insufficient Budgets): Holds regular swap meets to fill holes in collections by using each other's culls.

WWWL (World Wide Warrior Librarians): See above—International Association for Unemployable Librarians.

APPENDIX III

COMMON ABBREVIATIONS

AACR2: An Amazingly Complex Reference, too: Very thick book containing a set of rules for cataloging and also handy for pressing flowers.

ADDC: Abridged Diminution for Dummies to prevent Confusion: System used for generating smaller spine labels for patrons with limited numerical skills.

ACRL: A Club for Real Librarians: The biggest sector of the ALA (American Library Association).

BI: Bellowing Impotently: Method of teaching noisy, disinterested children how to use a library.

CLA: Club for Librarians Abroad.

CIP: Cute Information Page: Tiny writing found at the front of books.

CPU: Computer Part [That's] Unfathomable: Technical hardware that contains all the do-dads and widgets that make computers do all the stuff that they do.

DDS: Document Didn't Show: Used when fee paid to outside agency for printed or digital material failed to arrive when and where required.

DOS: Don't Overlook Something: A computer operating system for Windows-type machines that allows other things to happen.

DVD: Did (You) Vomit Development: One of the latest technological offerings, requiring the purchase of expensive equipment that will be obsolete in a few years.

Email: Electronic Menace Annoying Individuals and Libraries.

FAX: Feloniously Accessing X-rated Material: A communication medium whereby off-color jokes and pictures are transmitted to avoid any corporate digital filters.

FAQ: Frequently Antagonizing Queries: The types of unnecessary inquiries made by library patrons. For example, "Is this the library?" and "Can I speak to a librarian?"

FTP: Failure to Pay, as in a library fine.

HTML: Heck! This Muddles Librarians! Computer language used for writing library websites accessible to patrons who otherwise wouldn't visit libraries.

ISBN: Incredible System for Bibliomaniacal [k]Now-It-Alls: Secret code used by publishers for communcating with librarians.

LAN: Look! A Nastything: System whereby viruses can be transmitted from one computer to another without using disks or emails within a small area.

MARC: Mechanically, Actually Really Cool: A computer language that communicates between cataloger, library management software, and patrons. OK, forget the part about the patrons.

UNIMARC: Differentiates between the Marc on the library staff with graduate qualifications and the other Marc who doesn't.

URLs: Use Real Library Skills: For finding information on the Internet.

WAN: Watchout! Another Nastything: Similar to a LAN, but affecting a greater number of computers over a much larger geographic area.

X-REF: Censor's classification as not suitable for people under 18 years, unless Really Educated Fully.

APPENDIX IV

POLICE LINK-UP CODES FOR LIBRARIES IN ROUGH AREAS

Code 1: No particular hurry; whenever convenient
Code 2: Some urgency—get moving
Code 3: All-out emergency; lights and sirens
Code 4: Under control, no further assistance necessary

Code 5: Stakeout
Code 6: On foot; walking patrol
Code 7: Meal breaks
Code 8: Top brass in the building—look busy
Code 9: Industrial action—do very little

10–1: Receiving poorly
10–2: Receiving well
10851: Stolen book
11–79: Accident—ambulance is already en route
11–81: Accident—minor injury
11–82: Noninjury book cart collision
12–5: Having no valid borrowing card
14–6: Having a suspended borrowing card
22: (From 10–22) Cancel—forget it
26: (From 10–26) Clear; not stolen; no warrants of arrest outstanding
29: (From 10–29) To check a person or book for outstanding fines
36: (From 10–36) Clear to receive confidential information

203: Nonauthoritative information; next time, use a library book instead of asking the neighbor's eight-year-old kid for an opinion
204: No content; the pages have been removed from the book
205: Reset content; found the pages, glue them back in

400: Bad request; query not understood due to poor social or literacy skills
402: Payment required; unable to borrow until outstanding fines are cleared
403: Forbidden entry; closed stacks
404: Resource missing
406: Method not allowed; you have to officially borrow the book before leaving
409: Conflict; remove patron immediately
415: Physical fight; noise; disturbance; disorderly conduct

500: Internal error; ate curry for lunch and have to rush to bathroom
501: Command not implemented (remember to ask nicely next time)
502: Temporarily overloaded—come back later (say, next year)
503: Gateway time-out; the electronic security system isn't working
594: Vandalism—destroying property; graffiti
5150: Mentally disordered person that is an immediate danger to self/others (patron or library staff)

APPENDIX V

NEWSGROUPS FOR LIBRARIANS

alt.replacepage
Post a request for a copy of a page that has been torn out of a book. Usually the last page of a thriller or the Einstein page of an encyclopedia.

biz.publisherflyers
Can't find that one flyer for that one book you actually wanted, which arrived with the 2,357 pieces of junk mail for books you didn't want? Someone is bound to have kept it.

comp.complicatedstuff
Have a minor technical problem? Post a simple question to the list and receive an unending stream of responses you can't understand.

daemon.mailproblems
Does Daemon keep returning your email to you? Give him a piece of your mind about his service and receive yet another automated reply. This will prove how stupid he really is.

global.libraryarchives
Access the complete set of postings from all the library lists on the planet. Takes 19 hours to complete downloading of current day's archives. Don't forget to hit the reload button regularly to get the latest messages.

info.bloodyobvious
Broad spectrum of subscribers, from the raw novice to the highly experienced. Newbies ask simple questions, and libgeeks get to shatter fragile sensibilities with pompous replies.

k12.schoollibrarian
At the end of the usual chaotic day, ask the list why you even bother trying. There is always the chance, however small, that someone has the answer.

libraries.forsale
Find out what libraries are for sale in your area. New, used, reconditioned, established, or embryonic. Something for every budget. Finally, a way to be in charge of your own library—by owning it.

microsoft.youboughtit.tough
Complaints about Windows systems cheerfully ignored. Blue Screen of Death automatically launches on posting to this list.

no.org.here
Promotes the benefits of chaos. Swap anecdotes of mayhem in your library and feel less ineffectual compared to the ideals discussed in library school courses.

reality.check
Are you encumbered by grand visions of what your workplace could be? Drop a few lines in here, and you'll be brought back to Earth very quickly by those who have already tried it and failed.

soc.culture.librarians
Discuss with other librarians what makes librarians special. Open to nonlibrarians, but they don't get posting privileges ... they just read it and weep. Cruel, what?!

warrior.librarian
Pretend to have all the answers, talk tough, put on a great show of bravado, then slink quietly into work and do what you're told by people not fit to kiss your feet.

WARRIOR LIBRARIAN WEEKLY
IN THE CLASSROOM

Big Results for Small Change

In a world that makes absolutely no sense, staying on top of local and international affairs is essential.

Everything has a funny side. In recognition of this fact, *Warrior Librarian Weekly* is proud to invite your school to participate in our unique program—Warrior in the Classroom.

Through this special subscription offer, you can subscribe to *Warrior Librarian Weekly* for the reduced cost of just $200 per week. We know that this is a lot to pay for something so trivial, but it does contribute to the Warrior Librarian's Retirement Fund.

Issues in the News Online

Although we have no plans for an "Issues in the News" section, we can make up anything for the WLW in the classroom program. Schools that reach the target of just 300 subscriptions per week will receive a password that enables them to access this website, (which isn't password-protected anyway), news, features, and opinions published in the *Warrior Librarian Weekly* over the previous three months.

Not based on the professional media services archives, WLW is organized into fuzzy areas and misspelled indexes in ill-defined subject areas and employs a cheapskate search facility. Not a research tool, *Warrior Librarian Weekly* is available to every school library anyway.

For just $200 a week, participating students and teachers will have their own copy of the *Warrior Librarian Weekly* delivered directly to their computer via the Internet each day, if the network isn't "down," the computer actually works, and if you know how to operate it.

Monday through to Friday, a subscription provides one of the easiest ways for students to stay informed with the news, the views, and the opinions shaping our libraries. Each day, leading Warrior Librarians provide inaccurate reporting, shallow analysis, self-opinionated commentary, and pointless diversions.

With continuing changes to the curriculum, *Warrior Librarian Weekly* is a valuable "textbook" for many subjects, including:

- Libraries
- Librarians
- Librarianship
- Books
- Librarians in Books
- Books in Libraries
- Books on Librarianship
- Librarians in Libraries
- Librarianship Books in Libraries

CONTACT US

For further details or inquiries, please:
call toll–free, 1-800-S-T-U-P-I-D
email Biblia, the Warrior Librarian

WARRIOR LIBRARIAN
WEEKLY MERCHANDISE
Make A Budget Statement!

THE WLW BEANBAG
Discourage pointless lounging about with this attractive item for any library. Covered in steel-reinforced Kevlar and filled with broken lumps of concrete. Won't rot, rust, or split. Spray paint it yourself to match your library's decor or leave in natural colors to match your mood.

RRP: $159.95 + postage and packing $300.00

THE WLW COFFEE CUP
Comes prestained, chipped, and cracked to discourage borrowing. Colors: gray, murky brown, and puke yellow. "WLW" painted on side with liquid paper.

RRP: $12.95 + postage and packing $12.00

THE WLW PENCIL
Looks just like a regular pencil, but has "WLW" handwritten on quality recycled paper and attached with sticky tape. Very distinctive; for the discerning librarian.

RRP: $2.50 + postage and packing $3.00

THE WLW BOOKENDS
Unusual design, cleverly constructed to look like a house brick. Features the "WLW" logo in thick felt-tipped pen on one side only.

RRP: $0.50 each + postage and packing $5.00. Bulk discount available.

THE WLW T-Shirt
Stand out from the crowd at the next library conference! Quality Kmart fabric, with "WLW" in black high-gloss acrylic paint. White(ish) only. One size fits nobody.

RRP: $22.95 + postage and packing $10.00

About the Author

Amanda Credaro has been a geologist, veterinary nurse, research assistant, photojournalist, truancy officer, book reviewer, science teacher, e-zine publisher, and most lately a practicing Library Media Specialist. Her interests currently center on affective domain issues related to library use. Failures in life include pop-stardom (due to an inability to become anorexic) and housewife (due to an inability to stay on task). Living in Sydney, Australia, she is mother of 3 untidy but happy children and wife to the world's most tolerant husband.

About the Illustrator

Peter Lewis has been a taxi driver, pizza cook, laborer, ballet dancer, set designer, landscape painter, portrait artist, amateur philosopher, and book illustrator. He is currently engaged as the editorial cartoonist for the Newcastle Herald, Australia. His interests include pricking the egos of politicians, solving the world's problems, dreaming up weird ideas, and helping his ever-supportive wife, Theresa, raise their three beautiful daughters.